A
World
in Shadow

TRICENTENNIAL STUDIES, NUMBER 7

This volume is part of a series of *Tricentennial Studies,* published by the University of South Carolina Press on behalf of the South Carolina Tricentennial Commission, to commemorate the founding of South Carolina in 1670.

A
WORLD
IN SHADOW
The Free Black in
Antebellum South Carolina

Marina Wikramanayake

Published for the
South Carolina Tricentennial Commission
by the
UNIVERSITY OF SOUTH CAROLINA PRESS
Columbia, South Carolina

FIRST EDITION

Published in Columbia, S.C., by the
University of South Carolina Press, 1973

Library of Congress Cataloging in Publication Data

Wikramanayake, Marina.
  A world in shadow.

  (Tricentennial studies, no. 7)

  Bibliography: p.

  1. Negroes—South Carolina. 2. South Carolina—
History. I. Title. II. Series: South Carolina
Tricentennial Commission. Tricentennial studies,
no. 7.
  E185.93.S7W69   301.45'19'60730757   73–4437
  ISBN 0–87249–242–7

CONTENTS

TABLES

To My Mother
IRENE WIKRAMANAYAKE

ACKNOWLEDGMENTS

My FIRST YEAR IN THIS COUNTRY, IN WISCONSIN AND its Madison campus environment, provided little opportunity to observe the problem of race relations in the United States, although, as a student of American history, I was aware of its historical context. My interest in the subject developed during the first of many visits I made to the South.

I was returning from an international conference held in Williamsburg, Virginia, in 1963, and the Greyhound pulled up for a lunch-stop at a depot in Richmond. I was seated in the cafeteria when I noticed two lines to the food counter. One was composed of white people, the other of black. Those in the white line brought their food into the large, airy dining area in which I sat; the black line drifted into a dimly lit room beyond which I could not see. The lines were moving when a black soldier in uniform moved to the end of the line of whites. But in the next moment, sensing intrusion, he moved out and joined his fellow blacks in the other line. It was when he moved that I realized my own position in this strange ménage. It was not merely my sari that stuck out like a sore thumb in that section of the dining area. I summoned a waitress and inquired whether the place was segregated. "No," she assured me, "we desegregated last year." I realized how totally incongruous the word "integrated" would have been had she used it.

The scene I witnessed provoked some speculation on the

ix

nicely structured society to which I had recently been introduced in reconstructed Colonial Williamsburg. How effective were the delineations in antebellum Southern society and how enduring? Had there been aberrations, anomalies, momentary challenges—such as the black soldier I had seen—and how had Southern society responded to them? I returned to the University of Wisconsin with a new interest in the ramifications of slavery in the antebellum South.

Fortuitously, my adviser at the time was Professor Leon F. Litwack, who had recently published an incisive analysis of the free black in the antebellum North, *North of Slavery* (Chicago, 1961). We discussed the incident and I learned from him that such anomalies had, in fact, existed in the antebellum South. Chief among them had been the Southern free blacks. A study of these free Afro-Americans seemed an eminently feasible research project. However, the limited time I had as a foreign student in the U.S. made completion of the project a problem and I had to limit my horizons accordingly. About this time Professor Litwack left Wisconsin for the University of California, Berkeley, and my study came temporarily under the direction of Professor Avery O. Craven. On Professor Craven's advice I decided to confine my work to free blacks in South Carolina. (Studies on the free black in many of the Southern states had already been published; despite the sizable community of free blacks in the state and the reputation of its affluent members, South Carolina had been ignored.) Shortly afterward, Professor Richard Current became my adviser and the project was completed under his supervision.

My indebtedness to all three of my advisors is considerable. Professor Craven was more than helpful in securing access to research facilities in South Carolina. Professor

Current's willingness to give freely of his time and guidance enabled me to complete the project within the time limit I had set for myself. My debt to Leon Litwack can never be adequately assessed. He continued to guide and advise from Berkeley, and his assistance in the preparation of the manuscript for publication was invaluable. Any stylistic shortcomings and misinterpretation of facts are, of course, my own.

I am appreciative of the cooperation and the assistance afforded me by the staffs of the South Caroliniana Library, University of South Carolina; the South Carolina Historical Society, Charleston; the Charleston County Library; the State Historical Society of Wisconsin Library, Madison; the University of Chicago Library; the 135th Street Branch of the New York Public Library; and the Library of Congress. A very special acknowledgment is due to Mr. Charles E. Lee and his staff at the South Carolina Archives Department and Messrs. Leonardo Di Andrea and Harold De Lorme, consultant genealogists at the same institution. Their personal interest and assistance in my research was beyond the call of duty.

I owe a deep debt of gratitude to many individuals in Charleston whose insights into their own society gave me a better understanding of the subject I was dealing with. To list them here would be to risk making this preface lengthier than any single chapter of the book. I would, however, like to pay an especial tribute to the Reverend John T. Enwright, who was indefatigable in seeking out descendants of antebellum free Afro-Americans and making sure I obtained all the information I needed. This book owes a great deal to him. I am also grateful to Mesdames Naomi Johnston Brown, Irene Noisette, Julia De Costa, Mae Holloway Purcell, Anna Patrick and the late Miss Ella Small for permission to use material in their possession; and to Mr. T. Jayawardana who typed the manuscript in Ceylon for publication.

I am deeply grateful to Professor Nathan I. Huggins, of Columbia University, for the critical insights he has offered in the foreword to this book. Finally, my gratitude to my husband, Nalin Fernando, is immeasurable. As a journalist and a magazine editor, his experience and constant encouragement made the publication of this book an exciting endeavor.

Marina Wikramanayake
Santa Clara
February 12, 1973

FOREWORD

THE QUALITY OF CITIZENSHIP AND THE OPENNESS OF SO-ciety in America have not been preoccupations of American historians. Generally, it has been assumed that citizenship has been open to all born here and to those who have professed a commitment to the nation while demonstrating a minimal knowledge of its laws and institutions. Also, few would question the general thesis that the development of the American nation, from even before the Revolutionary crisis, was toward the openness of liberal capitalism and democracy and away from strictures and limitations on individual freedom.

Of course we have always known of the exceptions to the rule of American life. Slavery meant that a large number of people had no claim to citizenship. The status of Indians in this regard has always been perplexing. Furthermore, we have had to be aware that the maintenance of order—given the institution of slavery—forced antiliberal practices on Americans. Fugitive slave laws have to be considered anomalies in a free society.

However much we have been willing to take the exceptions into account, they have remained merely *exceptions* in our thinking. We have not been willing to define American life and history in terms of the experiences of those who have been excluded from the community of free men. American history has been seen as a story of whites (Anglo-Saxons at that) and free men. All others were peculiarities and their stories excepted from the major themes.

The character of all histories, however, is dependent on perspectives; a change in point of view can make every difference. The spirit of the last decade has compelled us to look at the American past through new and different eyes: those of blacks, women, Chicanos, Indians, and the "inarticulate." The challenge is formidable, but if good histories are forthcoming from the effort the reward will be a new American history that will be inclusive of the wide variety of human experience that has made it up.

Professor Wikramanayake has taken on a study of a subject that is crucial to the realization of that promise. The free black in the antebellum South has most often been discussed in terms of what he was not. He was not white, he was not a slave, he was not free, he was not a citizen, he was not an alien. He was the most striking peculiarity in a society that defined itself in terms of its "peculiar institution." But to know what he was not is to understand very little about him and the society of which he was part.

Professor Wikramanayake's study introduces us to the more complicated understanding of what free blacks were. We are shaken from the standard view that they were mainly a poor and pitiful lot. There were among them craftsmen and farmers, the educated and the propertied, and those with a modicum of power and prestige. They were important—perhaps indispensable—to the economies of the societies in which they lived. There were those who were cultivated, according to the standards of the time, as well as those who skirted the margin of acceptable civility.

Although free men, they were intimately tied to the institution of slavery. Except for a very few, they gained their status through some act of manumission or purchase through their own or friendly hands. In many ways, the definition of their status turned on their being black men who were not slaves. Yet, fundamentally, the free ground on which they stood was quite infirm. Kidnapping, court action, or impoverishment might undermine their free status into the mire of slavery. Free blacks were like no other Americans in this regard. Freedom and personal liberty were always for them tenuous, and the more precious because it was so.

From the perspective of free blacks, the American experience was quite removed from what we have come to know. Their history was one of more and more sharply defined limits rather than of developing horizons. As white Americans became more convinced that the society they wanted was to be a white society, they became more and more explicit in stipulating the distinctively confined role that non-whites were to play. Therefore, rather than sharing in the gains in personal freedom and liberty that we have associated with the emergence of the "common man" in the early nineteenth century, the free blacks found themselves suffering under greater and greater restraints. Citizenship rights such as voting, holding property, identity before the law, and freedom of movement were challenged or denied rather than recognized and expanded. As time went on, what might have been considered natural rights—to vote, to move, to prosper—were taken away. The very existence of a free black population was ultimately challenged by legal restrictions on manumissions and by promotions of colonization schemes. Indeed, it is not too extreme to say that, from the point of view of free blacks, the process of American development was from a relatively opened to an essentially closed society.

Considering the details of life for free blacks in the ante-

bellum South, America was a totalitarian society from
every point of view. Its primary and total commitment
was to the guarantee of a white society and to the maintenance of black slavery within it. Every other consideration had to conform to those ends. Free blacks thus
existed on a sufferance which grew more fragile as whites
became convinced that these fundamental objectives were
undermined by the former's very presence. It was not
merely that free blacks could be denied rights and treated
with contempt. Rather, it was that they had no real guar-
antees of any status. Their liberty would suffer or be sustained through the capriciousness of white men. Individual
free blacks depended on the influence and goodwill of
whites who favored them. But even that could not be certain when there were imagined threats to public peace.
The patrol system converted every white male into a military instrument to enforce the rule of white freedom and
black slavery. Modern totalitarian societies have shown
few improvements over the states of the antebellum South.
Emblematic of the totalitarian character of antebellum
South Carolina is the inquisition that followed the dis-
closure of the Denmark Vesey conspiracy. Here was no
testament of a society governed by law rather than men.
Here was no subservience of men to the rule of law and
principle. Rather, the trials testified to the willingness of
white men to use any means necessary to preserve the
whiteness of society and slavery within it.

Free blacks, nevertheless, survived and managed under
trying circumstances. They had little choice. Escape to the
North would have been slight improvement. While some
entertained the idea of expatriation to Africa, this too was
very problematic. The great majority chose to remain and
to try to work out some life for themselves. They quickly
learned, however, in the instance of the African Methodist

Episcopal Church, that segregation and community-building could be even more offensive to whites than any attempts at accommodation. They worked instead for self-definition through self-distinction. As free men, they were different from slaves, but wealth, property, education, church affiliation, voluntary associations, and skin color became means of finer distinctions of class. Pathetic, in many ways, nevertheless their efforts were intended to undermine the racist assumption that all blacks were alike. To the extent that distinctions could be recognized and honored, the possibilities of black improvement were enhanced. It may have been a futile hope, but it is one we can understand.

Recent studies of blacks in the North before the Civil War suggest that theirs was a different lot from their Southern brothers only in intensity, not in character. Demography and the institution of slavery caused Southern whites to be more direct and purposeful in their control of blacks than were Northerners. Everywhere in antebellum America, blacks were (to use Professor Wikramanayake's word) denizens rather than citizens. And everywhere, while the American society was opening to the "common man," it was closing to blacks. American history from their perspective is quite different from that we have come to accept.

In many ways, Afro-Americans have continued to be plagued by the predicament of their free black forebears. Neither slave nor free, citizen nor alien, blacks took up their role following emancipation. The early characteristics remain with us in many ways, however. Like the free blacks of the antebellum period, present-day Afro-Americans remain the source of the country's deepest problems and anxieties, and because of that they remain, for most, invisible men.

For many reasons, the continuum of the black experience in the United States to our own day is better understood by a study of free blacks than of slaves. It was their condition that the freedmen inherited following the Civil War. And, to a large extent, it was leadership from their population that attempted to direct the race's future in Reconstruction. It will be through their perspective that we will see a very important dimension of American history, that which has always been unfree and closed. Therefore, we can be most grateful to Professor Wikramanayake for this careful study of free blacks in antebellum South Carolina. For she takes us far along the way we must go.

Nathan Irvin Huggins
Columbia University
December 7, 1972

A
World
in Shadow

INTRODUCTION

OFFSHOOTS OF THE INSTITUTION OF SLAVERY, NEITHER slave nor free white, free blacks occupied an anomalous position in antebellum society. Within the state of South Carolina, the free black's position was never well defined. He was not recognized as a citizen per se but classified as a "denizen," who enjoyed limited rights.

While the antislavery crusade concerned itself mainly with the Southern slaves, the small community of free blacks attracted little attention outside the state until 1822, when the Denmark Vesey uprising, allegedly led by a free black, catalyzed a new crisis in the sectional issue between North and South. Unlike his counterpart in the North, the underprivileged free black of South Carolina was never able to press for an amelioration of his condition. His interest lay, rather, in maintaining the status quo. Any change in his condition would necessarily be adverse —a situation confirmed by the overriding sense of insecurity that the sectional issue generated among white Southerners. In the years immediately preceding the outbreak of the Civil War the legislature of South Carolina seriously considered the feasibility of enslaving its free colored population.

The free black community is of particular interest as a social phenomenon occupying a marginal position between

1

two societies, the slave and the white. Class stratifications within the group tended to produce a dual identity. In very broad terms, the mass of free blacks, whose daily contact was largely with the slaves, identified itself with the members of its race. A small group of wealthy, educated free blacks, however, sufficiently imbibed the norms of the predominant white society to identify itself, almost completely, with the white man. A lack of social mobility kept the two classes apart until after the Civil War, when the emancipation of the slaves created the opportunity for the black at the bottom of the ladder to attain the economic and social well-being of the free black elite. In the melting pot of postbellum South Carolina the blacks achieved a unity hitherto denied them by the ramifications of the slave system.

In the absence of viable social institutions, religion became the hub of the blacks' social life. The maintenance of separate black congregations brought the free black and slave into close proximity. Upper-class free black preachers, whose contact with the mass of blacks had been purely peripheral through organized acts of charity, found greater scope for their influence in the religious activity of black congregations. Emboldened by the prospects for unity, a group of free blacks established an independent African church in 1816, an unprecedented development in the history of the Southern black. The movement flourished despite repeated attempts by the authorities to suppress it. In 1822, however, rumors of a threatened insurrection presented a clear opportunity for a coup de grace. The African church was found to be the seat of the conspiracy, its class leaders were arrested and its founders were exiled. The Denmark Vesey affair had a significance for the free blacks well beyond the fact that its leader was alleged to be one of their number. Subsequent reprisals were mild.

The concerted attack on the African church revealed, rather, that the free black's freedom must necessarily conform to the subordination required by the slave system. Any deviation from that path, any hint of a growing independence would upset the social premises on which black slavery was founded.

CHAPTER I

"Free Persons of Color"

THE PECULIAR INSTITUTION PRODUCED A PECULIAR MAR-
ginal group in antebellum Southern society. Between
the well-defined states of master and slave there developed
a class of blacks whose freedom removed it from the con-
trols of slavery but gave it no access to the free society of
the master class. These "free persons of color," as Southerners denoted them,[1] were found in all the slave-holding
states of the South. Their numbers were greatest in Virginia and Maryland, and sizable free black communities
existed in North Carolina and Louisiana as well.[2] Smaller
in numbers, the free blacks of South Carolina were nevertheless a remarkable group. Within the confines of their
own society, they formed a microcosm of the larger, white
society; and in the successful reflection of the latter's norms

[1] The Northern black, classified in the United States census with the
"free colored population," was a very different phenomenon from his
brethren in the South, though subject to similar restrictions. For an incisive analysis of the Northern black's status in society, see Leon F. Litwack, *North of Slavery.*

[2] John Russell, *The Free Negro in Virginia;* James M. Wright, *The
Free Negro in Maryland;* John Hope Franklin, *The Free Negro in North
Carolina;* Rosser Howard Taylor, *The Free Negro in North Carolina.*

and institutions, they challenged the assumptions on which that society was founded.

Free blacks had existed in South Carolina since the early colonial period. Little is known of them during the first decades of the colony in the late seventeenth century, but the fact that the earliest slave code, in 1712, distinguished between "negroes and slaves" and defined the term "slave" reveals the presence of non-slave blacks.[3] It is likely that these free blacks found a special place in the missionary fold. In 1712, the Reverend Thomas Hasell, missionary of the Church of England's Society for the Propagation of the Gospel, recorded that he had twenty or thirty black men and women attending his Chapel of Ease, one of whom was free.[4] Later accounts of missionaries reveal a growing free black population and afford some evidence of their condition. In 1726 the Reverend Francis Varnod of St. George's Parish Winyah listed among his flock Robin Johnson, a free black, who had a wife and four children and owned nine slaves.[5]

The reaction of the slave-owner to the earliest form of missionary activity among the blacks was far from favorable, however, much of the hostility attaching to the possibility that the converted slave would be automatically entitled to the freedom espoused in the Christian faith.[6] It is no wonder, then, that the Reverend William Orr, whose lamentations on his "work of no small labour and difficulty" characterize his correspondence, wrote home to the S.P.G. in 1748 with much exultation that "Since my

[3] David J. McCord and Thomas Cooper, eds., *The Statutes At Large of South Carolina*, VII, pp. 360–65, hereinafter referred to as *Statutes At Large*.
[4] Frank J. Klingberg, *An Appraisal of the Negro in Colonial South Carolina*, p. 31.
[5] Ibid., p. 60.
[6] Ibid., p. 62.

last I have baptized two free nigroe Women after proper Instruction, both of them very sensible and sober. . . ."[7]

The free black's role in colonial society seems to have been of some significance. In 1739 the first of South Carolina's slave rebellions broke out in Stono, exciting considerable alarm among the white population and resulting in the passage of a severe slave code the following year.[8] Yet Frank J. Klingberg records that there was no subsequent decline in missionary activity among Afro-Americans, a factor he attributes to the healthy state of race relations deriving largely from miscegenation and a growing group of free blacks.[9] The free black appears to have acted as a buffer between the white and slave populations, mitigating the severity of slave control and serving to allay the fears of the white minority. Although he was on no terms of equality with the whites, his position was yet acceptable to them. There is no evidence, during this period, of attempts to either restrict or deprive the free black of his freedom.

Little is known of the origin of these first free blacks. Many of them, no doubt, were freed slaves. Slavery had not yet become an *économie dominante*,[10] and the concept of noblesse oblige may have operated strongly in favor of the slave. Records of wills in the colonial period reveal that manumission of slaves on the death of their owner was a widely accepted practice. James Gilbertson, who emanci-

---

[7] Ibid., p. 81.

[8] *Statutes At Large*, VII, pp. 397–417.

[9] *Negro in Colonial South Carolina*, pp. 69–70.

[10] Professor Andre Piettre makes a significant distinction between what he calls an *économie dominante*, or a ruling economy, which assumes such proportions that it virtually molds a culture, and an *économie subordonée*, or a subordinate economy, which is a factor rather than the dominant element in a way of life. The political and social ramifications of the institution of slavery in the nineteenth century tended to approximate the slave economy rather closely with the dominant, white economy. Andre Piettre, *Trois âges de l'économie*.

pated his slave by his will in 1720, made provision for her maintenance on his plantation.[11] The will of Sarah Fenwich in 1726 was less generous, insisting that the children of the freed slaves should be delivered to her heirs.[12] Whatever the varying conditions accompanying individual wills, manumission was often guaranteed a large number of slaves.

Some of the first blacks brought to the colonies were indentured servants who were freed at the expiration of their terms of service, like the white persons of this class.[13] This practice must have existed in colonial South Carolina, for there is evidence of it in the 1790s.[14] Free black immigration was also not uncommon, particularly in the coastal areas of Charleston, Beaufort and Georgetown. James Mitchell, later a prominent free black in antebellum South Carolina, was a Portuguese mulatto seaman who, finding conditions in Charleston more congenial, forsook the sea and became a landowner.[15] Close contact with the West Indies, also part of the British Empire, facilitated such settlement. Although migration was never on a large scale, as it was from Santo Domingo in 1794, the steady trickle contributed significantly to the increase of the free black population in the colonial period. In a time when marriage between black and white was accepted, large-scale miscegenation tended to create a discrete free mulatto group which continued to hold itself aloof from the free black masses in succeeding generations. By the outbreak

[11] Will of James Gilbertson, Record of Wills, Vol. 1, 1720–21 (Charleston County), pp. 49–50.
[12] Will of Sarah Fenwich, ibid., Vol. 2, 1722–31 (Charleston County), pp. 56–57.
[13] Carter G. Woodson, *Free Negro Heads of Families in the United States in 1830*, p. vi.
[14] Carlee McClendon, ed., *The First Federal Census, 1790, South Carolina: Edgefield County* (Columbia, S.C., 1959).
[15] The Holloway Scrapbook.

of the American Revolution there existed in the state a distinct, fairly well-knit group of free blacks who were able to survive in a well-established slave system and in large measure independent of the dominant white population.

Manumission had been the largest source of increase in the free colored population during the colonial period and continued to be the major source thereafter. Emancipation received a tremendous impetus during the American Revolution, inspired, no doubt, by the ideal of liberty which the colonists claimed to uphold in their quarrel with the mother country. It is pertinent to point out, however, that manumission was held out to the black, not as a right, but as a reward for faithful service, and, in more practical terms, as an inducement to continuing loyalty in the struggle with the British. When the country was relieved of the exigencies of that struggle and liberty had been enshrined for white citizens in the Bill of Rights, the ideal seemed to tarnish somewhat, and the rate of manumissions consequently declined.

A significant number of blacks continued to be manumitted between 1790 and 1840, however. In many cases the freed slaves were provided with land, capital or livestock, to enable them to earn a livelihood. In 1817 John Jackson bequeathed to his "faithful servant Elcy, Three Cows and Calfs and Three Sows to be allowed the liberty of Choice out of my Stock and $200 to be raised and levied out of my Estate . . . also my House and Landed Property during her life with Plantation Utensils and tools and Provisions, with some Bed Clothes and kitchen furniture and Poltry."[16] Cyrus Page, a former slave, had done so well since his emancipation that at his death he left a planta-

---

[16] Will of John Jackson, Record of Wills, Vol. 33, Book C, 1807–18 (Charleston County), pp. 1,331–33.

tion and five slaves to his children. His will mentions that one of his sons had been a slave and was now free. A grandson, Cyrus III, was still a slave, but there is reason to suppose that his freedom would also be procured since he belonged to the same owners.[17]

Manumission was effected by various means. While a majority of the freed slaves received their freedom on the death of their masters, a considerable number earned or bought their freedom. A remarkable case came before the courts when a suit for the freedom of Bill Brock was tried. It transpired in the evidence that not only had Brock operated as a free black with the consent of his master, but that he had even advanced the cash with which his master had purchased him.[18] Occasionally, the legislature manumitted slaves who had rendered distinguished services to the state. In 1822 two slaves whose evidence had led to the arrests made in the Vesey affair were awarded their freedom and an annuity by the South Carolina legislature.[19] One of them prospered enough thereafter to leave two houses and four lots of land in his will in 1854.[20]

The state's attitude toward manumission was not continuously favorable, however, and by 1841 severe legislation had effectively cut off its sources.[21] Still, within the first half of the nineteenth century manumissions contributed significantly to the increase in the free colored population and, to a large extent, conditioned its development as a recognizable class in society.

A much smaller segment of the population graduated

[17] Will of Cyrus Page, ibid., Vol. 16, Book A, 1774–79 (Charleston County).

[18] *Linam* v. *Johnson* (1831), in Helen T. Catteral, ed., *Judicial Cases Concerning American Slavery and the Negro*, II, p. 344.

[19] *Charleston Mercury*, Dec. 3, 1822.

[20] Will of Peter Desverney, Record of Wills, Vol. 49, Book B, 1856–62 (Charleston County), p. 866.

[21] This subject is discussed in Chapter II.

from slavery to freedom outside the regular procedure of manumission. It had been customary in colonial society for indentured servants to work their way to freedom. In post-colonial times the procedure acquired a new dimension. The first federal census for Edgefield County records the names of free blacks with the specified periods for which they were bound.[22] His period of service was usually contracted for, in order that the black might buy the freedom of a member of his family. Thus John Culclasher, a free mulatto bound for one year, might have been earning the freedom of his wife, while Frank, a free black bound for sixteen years, had probably to serve for both his wife and children.[23] The arrangement was extralegal and provided no guarantee of fulfillment. And, as sometimes happened, fate intervened to scatter the best-laid plans, as a free black discovered when he served seven years for his wife's freedom, only to record her death a month after his term was fulfilled.[24]

Conditions in the city of Charleston yielded a peculiar class of blacks who operated in a happy state of limbo, neither slave nor free. As increasing urbanization offered more opportunities for employment, it had been the practice of slaveholders in the cities to allow slaves to "hire their own time." By this means the slave craftsman worked independently, or for an employer, and the slaveholder received a commission on the slave's earnings. Such slaves were afforded a greater degree of laxity than was usual and often lived away from their owners.[25] Monday Gell, the chief witness for the state in the Vesey trials, was a slave

[22] McClendon, ed., *First Federal Census, Edgefield County.*
[23] Ibid.
[24] Interview with Leonardo di Andrea, genealogist, at the South Carolina Archives Department, Columbia, S.C., June 23, 1965.
[25] An excellent discussion of the position of quasi slaves can be found in Richard C. Wade, *Slavery in the Cities; the South, 1820–1860.*

craftsman and ran his own carpenter's establishment on Anson Street.[26] This group of quasi slaves enjoyed many of the practical advantages accruing to the free black. Their social intercourse was with the free colored population rather than with the slave, and their position was that of de facto free blacks. As manumission became progressively difficult and slaveholders began to circumvent the law by the practice of nominal slaveholding, the group grew.[27] Nor was the practice confined to Charleston. While city dwellers might gloss over infractions of the law in the interests of convenience, rural citizens frequently petitioned against the practice of slaves hiring their own time.[28] Yet, despite repeated regulations restricting the practice, this group of de facto free blacks continued to enjoy the privileges deriving from economic independence and identified themselves with the free colored group well beyond the Civil War.

Runaway slaves occupied a similar position in free black society. Their practical freedom was far more precarious, however, for they were subject to seizure at any given moment. However, when a fugitive slave succeeded in maintaining this freedom during his lifetime, his descendants were more secure in their status as free blacks. The fugitives tended to concentrate in urban areas where they were more likely to escape detection, but sizable fugitive slave communities, the populace of which were generally known in the South as Maroons, operated in a state of freedom in isolated outposts in the mountains and swamps of South Carolina. In June 1861, the *Marion Star* reported the discovery of such a group in a swamp outside the village.

[26] Document A, Documents Relating to the Denmark Vesey Uprising, 1822.

[27] *Supra.;* Chapter II.

[28] Petition of Elly Godbold and others of Marion, Petition of sundry residents of Orangeburg, in Petitions Relating to Slavery.

Provisions found in the camp indicated that the group had been there for at least some months.[29]

Almost half of the free black population in South Carolina was of mixed blood, or, as denoted in the United States census, mulatto. Interracial marriages had been acceptable in colonial society, and there was no law on the statute books of antebellum South Carolina which prohibited marriages between black and white. Yet social sanctions were strong in antebellum society and it is likely that a greater percentage of mulatto offspring was illegitimate. The racial breakdown of the colored population for 1850, given below, indicates the disparate number of mulattoes within the slave and free black population.

SOUTH CAROLINA COLORED
POPULATION—1850[30]

	Slave	Free
Black	372,482	4,588
Mulatto	12,502	4,372

While mulatto slaves formed 3.36 percent of the slave population, free mulattoes constituted 48.8 percent of the free black population.

The legal definition of the status of a child was based on Roman law, and the child's condition was therefore determined by that of his mother. Where miscegenation between the white master and black slave resulted in mulatto offspring, the child invariably became the slave of its father. However, it sometimes happened that Conscience reviewed the ruins of Pleasure, and consequent manumissions may account for the preponderant mulatto element in the free population. Cohabitation between white women

[29] *Marion* (S.C.) *Star,* June 18, 1861.
[30] J. D. B. De Bow, ed., *Compendium of the Seventh Census of the United States,* p. 83.

and black men was not unknown. In such cases the mulatto children followed the condition of the mother and were recognized as free. Court records of litigation involving the definition of color abound in cases where persons claimed they were the "descendants of a free white woman."[31]

The courts sometimes unwittingly added to the free colored population by consigning white persons of dubious origin to the degraded class of free blacks.[32] No degree of admixture was established for determining the status of a person of mixed blood, and court decisions were often erratic.[33] The nearest attempt at establishing a general principle was made by Justice William Harper in 1835: "The condition . . . is not to be determined solely by . . . visible mixture . . . but by reputation. . . . and it may be . . . proper, that a man of worth . . . should have the rank of a white man, while a vagabond of the same degree of blood should be confined to the inferior caste."[34] This definition necessarily entailed the further definition of "vagabond" and "a man of worth," but the learned judge evidently anticipated no difficulty on this score. Suffice it to observe that respectable mulattoes had better access to white society than their "vagabond" blood brothers.

Miscegenation was most common in urban and coastal areas, where the population was also most cosmopolitan. In 1860, blacks of mixed blood accounted for 25.2 percent

[31] Catteral, ed., *Judicial Cases Concerning Slavery*, II, p. 359; Petition of Sundry Inhabitants of Spartanburg and Union Districts On the Subject of Taxation in Petitions Relating to Slavery.

[32] Catteral, ed., *Judicial Cases Concerning Slavery*, II, pp. 317, 346–47, 491. The issue of color usually arose in three classes of cases—prohibition against inferior courts or the tax collector, objections to witnesses testifying in the superior courts, and actions of slander for words charging the plaintiff with being a mulatto.

[33] Ibid., pp. 346–47, 359.

[34] Ibid., p. 269.

of Charleston's population, while the rest of the state had only 5.15 percent.[35] Many of Charleston's most prominent free blacks were descendants of white citizens. Particularly outstanding was the Noisette family, which traced its lineage to a French horticulturalist, Philippe Stanislaus Noisette, himself a man of no mean heritage. Noisette migrated to Charleston from Santo Domingo in 1794, bringing with him his slave Celestine and her children. Many years later he petitioned the legislature for the emancipation of the children, declaring that he had "under peculiar circumstances become the father of six children begotten upon his faithful slave named Celestine."[36] Finding the legislature intractable, Noisette was compelled to provide in his will for the removal of his children from the state.[37] On his death, however, the family, which desired to enjoy the benefits of its inheritance, petitioned the legislature for permission for its members to remain in the state as free persons of color. The petition was supported by many of the best-known lawyers in Charleston, some of whom Noisette had appointed his executors.[38] Although no written evidence of the legislature's accession to the request is available, it was presumably granted, for the Noisettes continued in Charleston, maintaining the extensive farm on Rutledge Avenue which remained in the family until 1950.[39]

Many other prominent free blacks were of white ancestry. Francis Louis Cardozo, better known in postbellum politics, was the natural son of J. N. Cardozo, a Jewish

[35] E. Horace Fitchett, "The Origin and Growth of the Free Negro Population of Charleston, South Carolina," p. 423.

[36] Petition of Philippe Stanislaus Noisette, Botanist of Charleston, in Petitions Relating to Slavery.

[37] Will of Philippe Stanislaus Noisette, Record of Wills, Vol. 40, Book A, 1834–39 (Charleston County), pp. 203–4.

[38] Petition of Alexander Noisette and others, Noisette Papers.

[39] Ibid.; interview with Mrs. Irene Noisette, Charleston, July 14, 1965.

businessman who had settled down in Charleston.[40] Richmond Kinloch, a wealthy millwright, was of Scottish descent and had many relatives living in Charleston, descendants of the Kinloch brothers who originally migrated to Charleston.[41]

Miscegenation among Indians and blacks was not uncommon. In such cases, if the mother was an Indian, the child was not only free but also exempt from many of the restrictions imposed on free blacks.[42] For the most part, however, this group was absorbed into the free colored population and operated within the free black society. Richard and Joseph Dereef, both descendants of a free Indian woman, were wealthy speculators in real estate, pillars of the free black community, and senior members of the Brown Fellowship Society, Charleston's foremost free black organization.[43]

While the white citizenry contributed in no small measure to the increase of the free colored population, cohabitation within the free black community resulted in an equally significant increase. If a black mother was free, the children of a slave father were considered free. The institution of marriage was developed among free blacks at all levels. Family trees of the free black elite attest to this fact, while church records of baptisms provide evidence of legitimate parentage among the humbler members of free black society.[44] The following table was drawn from the register of the Episcopal Church of Prince George Winyah,

[40] William J. Simmons, *Men of Mark*, pp. 428–31; James S. Pike, *The Prostrate State*, p. 35.

[41] Interview with Mrs. Julia De Costa, Charleston, S.C., July 17, 1965.

[42] Appendix B.

[43] Register of Mesne Conveyance, B-12, pp. 598–600, 250–52, Q-13, pp. 121–22, X-13, pp. 46–47, 73, H-13, p. 633; Diary of Richmond Kinloch; Holloway Scrapbook.

[44] D. E. Huger Smith and A. S. Salley, Jr., eds., *Register of St. Philip's Church*.

1813–1916, which distinguishes between whites, free blacks and slaves.

BAPTISMS OF THE EPISCOPAL CHURCH
OF PRINCE GEORGE WINYAH[45]

Parents	Child	Date of Baptism
Benjamin & Ann London	Benjamin	March 11, 1815
George & ——— Mitchell	Isaac Daniel	November 11, 1815
Richard & Susannah Nites	Isabella	September 22, 1822
——— Brodnt	Hagar	——— 1824
Richard & Susannah Nites	Sarah	——— 1824
Richard & Susannah Nites	Betty	December 20, 1825
John & ——— Hall	Thomas Daniel	July 19, 1829
Richard & Susannah Nites	Thomas Thisbe	December 13, 1829
Sary & Scipio Bertus	———	April 11, 1831
Scipio & Thomas	———	March 13, 1831
Phillis & Sary	———	April 6, 1831
Scipio & ——— Thomas	———	May 22, 1831
——— Ingliss	———	April 20, 1836

The natural increase within the free colored population was of particular importance after 1841, when all other avenues of entry into free black society, except birth, were closed. In 1850 only two slaves were officially manumitted in the state of South Carolina.[46] In the same year, of a total of 8,960 free blacks, only 142, or 1.59 percent, had been born within the United States and outside South Carolina, and had probably entered the state before restrictions were imposed on free black immigration.[47] In the latter half of the antebellum period, any increase in the free colored population came strictly from within the group. Population figures for this period show a steady decline in the

---

[45] Register of the Episcopal Church of Prince George Winyah, 1813–1916.

[46] De Bow, Compendium of the Seventh Census, p. 64.

[47] Ibid., pp. 78–79.

increase rate and may be explained by the preponderance of women among free blacks.

Before 1820, immigration accounted for a considerable portion of the free colored population. The decade of the 1790s brought a wave of immigration when the successful slave rebellion in Santo Domingo dispossessed a host of hapless whites, family-bound slaves and disenchanted free blacks. The influx of the last group seems to have been considerable, for it excited a good deal of alarm within the native white population, particularly in Charleston, where blacks tended to concentrate. In July 1794, "Rusticus"[48] warned in the *Columbian Herald* that "an excess of humanity [for the Santo Dominicans] has led us to be totally blind to our interests and that mindful alone of their situation, we have forgot the dangers of our own."[49] About the same time a meeting of white Charlestonians called for the expulsion of all blacks who had migrated from the French West Indies within the last three years.[50] The legislature appears to have shared the excitement, for in the same year an act was passed prohibiting the entry of free blacks from any port in the western hemisphere.[51]

Immigration from the other Southern states continued, however, and such immigrants were usually accepted without much ado. Eaton Fetlister, a free black from Delaware, by a long series of misfortunes found himself carried as a slave to Alabama, where he escaped. Arriving in South Carolina, the towering black—he was seven feet tall—inevitably attracted attention and was apprehended as a runaway slave.[52] The sequel to the arrest is not known, but if

[48] The letter was attributed to Alexander Garden, missionary among the blacks and rector of St. Philip's Church.
[49] Letters of "Rusticus," 1794.
[50] Ibid.
[51] *Statutes At Large,* VII, pp. 431–32.
[52] *South Carolinian* (Columbia) , Nov. 20, 1838.

Fetlister was able to prove that his free status had been accepted in Delaware, the state of South Carolina would have recognized him as a free black. A similar case came before the courts in 1803, when a black named Ben produced records of his freedom in Virginia and was legally recognized as a free black in South Carolina.[53]

As laws against free blacks became more repressive in other Southern states, the influx of free blacks into South Carolina increased.[54] Immigration from 1810 to 1820 reached such proportions that, at the end of the period, Governor John Geddes called for "the strongest measures to prevent it," with the further admonition that "it may be deemed a duty to oppose at the *threshold* everything likely in its consequences to disturb our domestic tranquillity."[55] The year 1820 was particularly unlucky for the free black. Not only did the legislature comply with the governor's request, but in its zeal to preserve domestic tranquility it also passed an omnibus law which outlawed manumission (save by legislative act), forbade immigration on the pain of enslavement, and imposed strong restrictions on the egress and ingress of free blacks.[56] These security measures apparently did not suffice. In the Denmark Vesey scare which gripped the state two years later,

[53] Miscellaneous Records, Book Q, p. 60; Catteral, ed., *Judicial Cases Concerning Slavery*, II, p. 283.

[54] Between 1805 and 1810, Maryland disfranchised and prohibited the immigration of free blacks and imposed restrictions on free blacks engaged in commercial activity; Virginia in 1813 imposed a poll tax on all free blacks; Tennessee required the registration of all free blacks in 1806 and forbade interracial marriages in 1822; Louisiana prevented the immigration of free blacks in 1807. In Georgia, a law in 1811 provided for the sale of free blacks for certain crimes, while in 1818 the free colored population was deprived of the right to hold real estate or slaves. Woodson, *Free Negro Heads of Families*, pp. xxiv–xxv; Edward Forrest Sweat, "The Free Negro in Ante-bellum Georgia," p. 112.

[55] Howell Meadows Henry, *Police Control of the Slave in South Carolina*, p. 178.

[56] *Statutes At Large*, VII, pp. 459–61.

attention was called again to the large numbers of free black immigrants. When sanctions on the free blacks were considered, Gov. Thomas Bennett suggested the alternative of expelling all recent free black immigrants.[57] The suggestion was not adopted, but the vigilance maintained after 1820 was effective in sealing off the state to free black immigration.

A stranger visiting Sumter County today may come across a baffling breed called "Turks." In recent years these Turks, known also as "Free Moors," have claimed and received recognition as white citizens.[58] Their status in antebellum South Carolina was less clear, and their origin has been the subject of much speculation. So meager are the facts relating to them that the wildest conjectures, based on what must surely be flights of fancy and geographical ignorance, have been advanced to support their origin. One tale finds them to be "nobles of the Delhi court," who brought with them "the golden women of the East who came ashore with the Red Sea Men when they beached the pirate ship *Loyal Jamaica* [?] in Bulls Bay [South Carolina]."[59] The most commonly accepted explanation of their origin is that two "foreigners," Joseph Benenhaley and a man named Scott, served General Thomas Sumter during the Revolutionary War and later settled on the general's plantation.[60] In 1790, the family, "sundry free Moors, subjects of the Emperor of Morocco and resident in this state," petitioned the legislature that "they be tried under the

[57] Document A, Documents Relating to the Denmark Vesey Uprising.
[58] Papers Relating to the Free Moors of South Carolina.
[59] Herbert Ravenal Sass, "Carolina's Pirate Coast," *Holiday Magazine* (April 1954) , pp. 137–39, in the South Carolina Archives Department.
[60] Very likely Benenhaley and Scott sired the Moors. General Sumter discovered the two when he was recruiting troops. Benenhaley was a "Caucasian of 'Arab' descent." Scott was "thought to be partly of French descent and had an assumed name." T. S. Sumter, *Stateburg and Its People*, pp. 68–70; Anne King Gregorie, *History of Sumter County*, pp. 467–68.

same laws as the citizens of this state . . . and not under the Negro Acts." The petition was granted.[61] Yet the census for Sumter District in 1830 lists as free blacks Elizabeth Benenhaley, Aaron Oxendine, William Chavers, Thomas Chavers, Randel Oxendine, Josiah Scott and many others of the same family.[62] It is possible that this group, while holding aloof from the black population, was sometimes confused with the latter on account of its complexion. Members served in white regiments in the Civil War and have since maintained an identity distinct from the blacks.[63]

In 1790 the free black population of South Carolina totaled 1,801.[64] Over half of this number was concentrated in the city of Charleston and its environs. As a seaport of some importance, Charleston maintained a steady intercourse with the rest of the world and was also the center of immigration from abroad. Its population was consequently more cosmopolitan, and, from the closeness with which all races were thrown together in a restricted urban area, there developed a relationship between black and white that was atypical of the state at large. The slave population of the city was comprised of a large number of house slaves and artisans who were afforded a greater degree of laxity than the plantation field hands of rural South Carolina. Their position in Charleston was less anomalous and their status more acceptable than it was in other parts of the state, not excepting Columbia, South Carolina's capital and second city. Charleston's free blacks benefited by this breadth in outlook. Free blacks there enjoyed privileges and opportunities that were denied their

---

[61] Gregorie, *History of Sumter County*, p. 468.
[62] Woodson, *Free Negro Heads of Families*, p. 159.
[63] Confederate Muster Rolls; Papers Relating to Free Moors.
[64] *First Federal Census of the United States.*

rural counterparts. They were able to develop their own institutions, participate widely in the economic life of the city and, in some very outstanding cases, rise to positions of prominence and affluence in the community.[65] The very size of the free black population contributed in large measure to its position, for it was impossible to ignore its numbers. In addition, the relatively cosmopolitan outlook of the city gave black members a better opportunity, at all levels, to earn a livelihood and to fulfill themselves as far as the peculiar institution would allow.

It was therefore natural that free blacks in the state should flock to the peninsula. To a lesser extent, this was true of the other coastal districts of Georgetown and Beaufort. After 1830, the census reveals a decline in the rate of increase of the free black population for the state. The figures for the coastal areas remained steady, however, and immigration from other parts of the state continued to add to the maritime population as the table below indicates.[66]

	South Carolina	Charleston District	City of Charleston	Beaufort	George-town
1790	1,801	950	586	153	113
1800	3,185	1,161	951	205	95
1810	4,554	1,783	1,472	181	102
1820	6,826	3,615	1,475	181	227
1830	7,921	3,627	2,117	507	214
1840	8,276	3,201	1,558	462	188
1850	8,960	3,861	———	579	201
1860	9,914	3,622	3,785(?)	809	183

[65] Conditions among free blacks in Charleston are discussed at length in E. Horace Fitchett, "The Free Negro in Charleston, South Carolina" (Ph.D. diss., University of Chicago, 1950). Fitchett's study is sociological rather than historical, but it vividly portrays the position of the free black in his society. I am indebted to the author for the many clues to primary sources which aided the research involved in my own study.

[66] Federal Census of the United States, 1790–1860.

Geographical factors determined the distribution of the free black population to a very limited extent, and here too settlement seemed to follow the pattern of white settlement rather than the contours of the land. As with the white population, the largest concentration of free blacks was in the tidewater area, and Charleston, Beaufort and Georgetown continued to be the centers of settlement throughout the seventy-year period under consideration. The lower pine belt,[67] also known as the "pine barrens" on account of its sandy, poorly drained soil, was always sparsely settled. While the white population was inconsiderable, the slave population was always large in proportion, indicating that the region was dominated by a plantation economy. The free black, unlike the slave, had a choice of settlement, and population figures reveal a very limited distribution of free blacks in the area. Williamsburg County is a case in point. The population in 1800 was a mere four, expanding to forty-seven in 1810, and reaching a peak of fifty-seven in 1820. Thereafter a portion of the population seems to have emigrated, for the numbers dwindled to twenty-six in 1830, growing very slowly to reach forty-three in 1860.[68] The figures for Marion County are somewhat higher, but the county extended down to the coast and it is likely that a greater part of its population was concentrated in the coastal tip.

The upper pine belt showed around 1820 an increase in free black population which was maintained until the 1840s. Figures for Orangeburg, which list 170 free blacks in 1790, fluctuate violently until 1810 when a steady increase is discernible. The free black population here grew from 331 in 1820, to 425 in 1830, reaching a peak in 1840

[67] Appendix A.
[68] *Federal Census of the United States.*

with 699, after which a slight decline set in.[69] Within the
area, Barnwell County, close to the Georgia border, appears to have had the largest concentration of free blacks.
The figures for Richland are closely parallel, irrespective
of the fact that the growth of the district was conditioned
by the development of the city of Columbia. Free blacks
here tended to live in the rural environs of Columbia
rather than within the city.[70] It is likely that this westward
migration, which began in the 1820s, had its sources in the
lower pine region rather than in the tidewater area, for
where the figures for the latter remain constant, the numbers in the former seem to decline.

Free black settlement in the piedmont region, like the
corresponding white settlement in the area, did not develop until the 1830s. Within the region, the largest area
of settlement appears to have been in Abbeville County,
in the lower Saluda valley. Beginning with a negligible 27
in 1790, the free black population averaged around 64 in
the 1820s, shot up to 172 in 1830 and continued to increase. In 1840 there were 323 free blacks in the county, a
figure which grew to 357 in 1850 and 367 in 1860.[71] The
rapid development of white plantations in the area is
evinced by the growing slave population. In 1790 Abbeville County had 1,665 slaves, 8,829 in 1820, 13,106 in 1830
and 20,500 by 1860.[72] The western limits of the piedmont
region possessed a very small free black population until
1860, when an outflow from Abbeville County appears to
have settled in Spartanburg and Greenville.[73]

In the city of Columbia the settlement of free blacks
appears to have been very slow and affords no comparison

[69] Ibid.
[70] Ibid.
[71] Ibid.
[72] Ibid.
[73] Ibid.

with Charleston. In 1830, of 499 in Richland District only 90 lived in Columbia.[74] Economic opportunity was not lacking, for there is evidence of free black carpenters, bootmakers and independent tradesmen in the city.[75] But free blacks in the district were mostly small farmers in rural areas.[76] It would be reasonable to assume that the development of the city of Columbia had little impact on free black settlement. Richland District continued to have the same proportion of free blacks as the neighboring midland counties of Newberry and Sumter.

Coincidences in the distribution of slave and free black populations in the census of 1790 suggest only the merest outline of a pattern of settlement. The profitability of slavery had not yet been impressed upon the people of South Carolina to the degree it was after 1800, and slave populations were not as widely distributed through the state as they were after this period. The lines of settlement tend to be clear, and some patterns can therefore be drawn based on the beginnings of large-scale slave labor and the settlement of free blacks in South Carolina. The tidewater region, however, affords no key to the general pattern of settlement, for while slave labor was found to be profitable in the rice fields of the swamps, economic opportunities in urban centers and fishing communities continued to draw a considerable number of free blacks to the area.[77] Early settlement in the midlands and in the piedmont region, on the contrary, shows some general pattern. The settle-

[74] *Fifth Federal Census of the United States.*

[75] Petition of James Patterson, in Petitions Relating to Slavery; *South Carolinian* (Columbia), Mar. 10, 1847.

[76] Unpublished Agricultural Schedules of the Seventh Census of the United States.

[77] As early as 1731, John Primas, a free black, bought a hundred acres of land in the Beaufort area for a hundred pounds sterling. It is very likely that the land was cultivated by slave labor. Memorials, Vol. 4, p. 436, in manuscripts of the South Carolina Archives Department.

ment of Orangeburg is particularly revealing. Southern
Orangeburg was settled around 1735. Its inhabitants were
largely Swiss immigrants who formed a compact settlement
of small farmers, many of whom were indentured servants,
earning their title to their small holdings. Between 1730
and 1765 only twelve blacks were listed in the settlement.[78]
In 1790 free blacks constituted 10 percent of the black
population in the area.[79] Northern Orangeburg, on the
other hand, yielded a different economy. Here cattle
ranges constituted the wealth of the area and large land-
holdings were common. There is evidence of slave labor on
a relatively large scale, and the cultivation of 1,000-acre
tracts of land was not uncommon.[80] In 1790 northern
Orangeburg listed only 21 free blacks, in comparison with
the southern section, which had 149.[81]

Free black settlement in what was later Abbeville
County was always considerable and dates back to an early
period. In 1752 Mathew Chavous, a free person of color,
applied for a warrant for 300 acres of land, claiming he
had lived twelve years in the province. The governor's
council was undecided "whether the giving away of lands
to Negroes in this Province and to their Posterity be Expedient."[82] The issue seems to have been settled in the
black's favor, for John Chevis, a free black carpenter (one
of the many Virginians settling the area) applied for land
and received a favorable hearing from the governor and
council, who merely stipulated that he prove his freedom.[83]
The development of a plantation economy in the area does
not appear to have really got under way until 1830.[84]

[78] Robert L. Meriwether, *The Expansion of South Carolina*, p. 45.
[79] *First Federal Census.*
[80] Meriwether, *Expansion of South Carolina*, pp. 48–49.
[81] *First Federal Census.*
[82] Meriwether, *Expansion of South Carolina*, p. 128.
[83] Ibid., p. 133.
[84] *Fifth Federal Census.*

The rapid development of a slave economy after 1800 and its widespread distribution tend to blur the lines of settlement, and it is hardly possible to draw a cohesive pattern in the distribution of slave and free populations in the nineteenth century. At most, a coincidence of the two is discernible, and it is possible that the free black communities of the large slaveholding areas derived from the slave population. In the piedmont region, where free black migration followed white settlement, the coincidence is strongest but provides no basis for any generalization.

Population changes on the North Carolina and Georgia frontiers are of some interest as an index to the condition of South Carolina's free blacks. On the whole, North Carolina was the most liberal of the Southern states in its attitude towards the free black,[85] and it is likely that there was considerable emigration to North Carolina from the counties on its southern border. Population figures are not very helpful in indicating this movement, however, partly because the returns for some of the South Carolina counties are very inaccurate. Statistics for Lancaster County (adjacent to Anson County in North Carolina), for instance, are too fantastic to be credible. From 68 in 1790, the figure drops to 38 in 1800, only to zoom to 372 in 1810, leaving one with the wildest conjectures about the birthrate among Lancaster free blacks, since neither its slave population nor that of Anson County or any of the surrounding counties in South Carolina shows any loss in population for the year.[86] Counties in North Carolina bordering the Palmetto State were Mecklenburg, Anson, Richmond, Robeson and Brunswick; the corresponding counties in South Carolina were, in the same order, Chester and York, Chesterfield and Lancaster, Marlboro, Liberty and Horry. In a comparison of statistics for the respective counties,

---

[85] Franklin, *Free Negro in North Carolina, passim.*
[86] *Federal Census.*

Richmond and Marlboro alone provide an index to population movements as the table below indicates:

County	1800	1810	1820	1830	1840	1850	1860[87]
Richmond, N.C.	25	22	57	153	336	225	345
Marlboro, S.C.	179	84	147	55	102	156	168

If the returns for Marlboro County are to be accepted,
a significant decrease occurred between 1820 and 1830,
while a corresponding increase took place in the same decade in Richmond County. Allowing for the fact that this
increase may have been caused by internal factors within
North Carolina, the possibility that some of it came from
South Carolina is not to be overlooked. The omnibus act
of 1820, which imposed severe restrictions on free persons
of color, would, in all likelihood, have induced the free
black to seek relief by emigrating.

A similar movement is discernible on the Georgia frontier. Edward Forrest Sweat records that the greatest source
of increase in the free black population of Georgia was
immigration, and that in Richmond and Burke counties,
in particular, the largest number came from South Carolina.[88] Both counties were on the South Carolina border,
across the Savannah, and migration may have been facilitated by the ferry across the river in Edgefield County and
at what is now Augusta, Georgia. In Georgia, moreover,
native free blacks were allowed to leave, temporarily, "to
go to an adjoining State."[89] This may well account for the
concentration of free blacks in Edgefield County, South
Carolina. While South Carolina legislation made such ingress impossible after 1820, it is very likely that South

---

[87] Ibid.
[88] "Free Negro in Ante-bellum Georgia," p. 3.
[89] Ibid., p. 4.

Carolina free blacks made use of this provision in the Georgia law to "reenter" Georgia. Statistics for Richmond and Burke counties for this decade show a considerable increase in free blacks who may have come from South Carolina. Figures for adjoining Aiken or Winton counties in South Carolina are not available. Although figures for Edgefield County bear out the trend to some extent, the violent fluctuation in numbers warns that they be treated with caution. The table below indicates the pattern of movement:

County	1800	1810	1820	1830[90]
Richmond, Ga.	54	26	110	235
Burke, Ga.	14	76	84	125
Edgefield, S.C.	61	151	57	203

The pattern is by no means conclusive, but there is some evidence that emigration to Georgia continued after 1830. Sweat records that in 1850, of 2,931 free blacks in the state, 215 had been born outside Georgia, and 105 of them had their nativity in South Carolina. In 1860, of 3,500 free blacks in Georgia, 225 were born elsewhere, and 122 of this number were born in South Carolina.[91] A minimum of 17 must therefore have emigrated within the decade, a trend supported by the increasing pressure exerted on the free black in South Carolina in the decade of the 1850s.[92]

The growth of South Carolina's free black population between 1790 and 1860 was uneven, both in numbers and in distribution. Between 1790 and 1800 the population almost doubled, continuing to grow more steadily until 1830, when it reached its peak. Thereafter, a decline ap-

[90] *Federal Census.*
[91] Sweat, "Free Negro in Ante-bellum Georgia," pp. 6–7.
[92] *Supra.;* Chapter VIII.

pears to have set in. The rate of increase fell from 16.04 in 1830 to 4.48 in 1840; although it improved in the next two decades, averaging 8.26 in 1850 and 10.64 in 1860, the rate of increase contrasted strongly with that of the earlier decades which had averaged 49.89 in 1820 and 76.84 in 1800.[93] The increase during the period 1850–60 was confined to births within the population, additions from without being effectively sealed off by legislation. The fact that the free blacks during this period constituted an older age group, with an unfavorable sex ratio, tended to keep the rate of increase low.[94] In addition, migration to the Northern states, Canada and Liberia had the effect of draining the population somewhat, though not to a really significant degree.

In 1860, free blacks numbered 9,914, or 1.4 percent of the total population, and, in terms of numbers, the group had never been of much significance. As a marginal community occupying an anomalous position in Southern society, however, South Carolina's free blacks present a challenging testimony to sheer survival in adversity. In their response to the environment imposed upon them, they themselves constituted an integral part of Southern society.

[93] De Bow, *Compendium of the Seventh Census,* p. 64.
[94] *Federal Census.*

CHAPTER II

The Politics of Manumission

THE GROWTH OF THE FREE BLACK POPULATION IN SOUTH Carolina depended largely on the facility with which manumission could be accomplished. While manumission was the major source of increase in the free colored population, the manner in which it was carried out also had a direct bearing on the condition of freedom. A master emancipating an aged slave might, in reality, be ridding his household of a burden and turning loose into free society a person totally unequipped for freedom. On the other hand, slaves manumitted by the wills of their masters might be provided with the means of support and, in some measure, prepared for free status. Thus the will of John Oxendine in 1797 stipulated that his "Negro boy Bill be put to a trade at sixteen and at twenty-five be freed."[1]

An outstanding case of manumission with economic support is that of Hannibal Dearington. Freed by his owner's will, the slave inherited a share in his master's plantation and an annual allowance of £15 sterling for his services as overseer.[2] Dearington's subsequent success in assimilating

[1] Will of John Oxendine, Record of Wills, Vol. 26, Book B, 1793–1800 (Charleston County), pp. 581–82.

[2] Will of Hannibal Dearington, ibid., Vol. 28, Book A, 1800–07 (Charleston County), pp. 3–4.

the norms of the white society is evident in his own will. Convinced, no doubt, of the efficacy of sound investment, he provided that the money accumulated from his share in the plantation "be laid out in the purchase of as many young Negro Women as the different sums consolidated will buy and them to be put on shares or hired out to the best advantage." The income derived was to pay for the freedom of his daughter and two sons, who were to be educated and taught "the use of figures as far as the rule of three." To his less-fortunate wife, who was to remain a slave, he willed an annual allowance of ten pounds of coffee and twenty pounds of sugar, in the hope, one suspects, of sweetening her servitude![3]

Conditions under which manumission was granted did not depend solely upon the good relationship between master and slave. As long as the slave remained the property of his owner, there could be little interference with the latter's inviolable right of private property. But when the slave assumed the capacity of an individual and entered free society, the legislature, as custodian of that society, assumed control over his person. Extending the argument, the legislature claimed the right to prescribe the conditions in which the slave could be admitted into free society. Manumission thus came under strict legislative control.[4] To be sure, the same degree of control operated in legislative restrictions on immigrant free blacks and on the activities of freeborn blacks within the state, but while such restraints acted to limit the extent of their freedom, their initial claim to freedom was never denied. In exercising the power to control manumission, the legislature, in effect, imposed a judgment on the black's capacity for freedom.

[3] Ibid.
[4] J. D. Wheeler, *Laws of Slavery* (New Orleans, 1837), p. 387.

It is possible to trace four stages in the development of state policy toward manumission, coinciding roughly with the passage of three major laws. In 1790 the practice of manumission continued in the tradition of the pre-Revolutionary era. Essentially a contract between master and slave, manumission required no official sanction, although a certificate of freedom might accompany the transaction for the convenience of the freed slave.[5] Many slaves bought their freedom. The cash value of freedom varied with the relationship between master and slave. A slave might hire out his own time, paying his master a regular commission on his earnings until he made up the sum originally paid for him, or he might be obliged to pay a higher price for his freedom to insure that both master and servant derived some benefit from the transaction. In many cases the slave "purchased" his freedom for a nominal sum, as the slaves of John Bostick did in 1800 when they received their freedom "in consideration of the sum of $10."[6]

Large numbers were manumitted by the wills of owners during this period. In 1797 Joseph Wigfall, a planter residing in Charleston, provided for the emancipation of nine slaves at his death, with an injunction to his executors that the freed slaves be allowed to reside on his plantation.[7] In many instances the generosity of the owner appears to have generated a similar spirit among the recipients of his bounty. Anne King Gregorie records the case of a freed slave who inherited a life interest in twenty acres of land in 1783. A few years later he had prospered enough

[5] Certificate of Freedom, from Joseph Bell, planter of St. John's Parish, to Nancy, his faithful servant, and her child Jacob, in Miscellaneous Records.

[6] Manumission of Judah, a slave, by John Bostick, in Miscellaneous Records, Book B, p. 155; Manumission of James, a mulatto slave, ibid., pp. 186–87.

[7] Will of Joseph Wigfall, Record of Wills, Vol. 28, Book A, 1800–07 (Charleston County), p. 45.

to buy two slaves, a woman and a child whom he eventually emancipated in 1791.[8] Manumission appears to have become so much an adjunct of the institution of slavery that when Caesar, a slave, discovered a cure for rattlesnake bite in 1780, it seemed only natural that the legislature reward him with emancipation.[9] A few years later Ariel, whose feat of courage in extinguishing a fire in St. Philip's Church is still a legend among Charleston's blacks, received his freedom in recognition of his services.[10]

In the absence of any rules prescribing the procedure for manumission, de facto manumission was widely accepted and rarely challenged. In 1797, in *Snow* v. *Callum,* Chief Justice Hugh Rutledge ruled that evidence of the intention to emancipate on the part of the slaveholder was sufficient to establish the freedom of a black.[11] While this may not have been the order of the day, Justice John Belton O'Neall recalled that "Before the Act of 1800 . . . anything which showed that the owner had deliberately parted with his property and dissolved the *vinculum servitii,* was enough to establish freedom."[12]

The Act of 1800 represents the first attempt at legislative interference with private manumission. Its intention was to regulate rather than restrict manumission and its preamble reveals the circumstances which brought about legislative regulation. "Whereas, it hath been a practice for many years past in this State, for persons to emancipate or set free their slaves, in cases where such slaves have been

8 Anne King Gregorie, *History of Sumter County,* p. 131.

9 Francois, Alexander du Frederic, Duke de la Rouchefoucault-Liancourt, *Travels Through the United States of America, the Country of the Iroquois, and Upper Canada in the Years 1795–1796, and 1797,* p. 595.

10 Edward G. McCrady, *An Historic Church,* pp. 35–36; *Charleston Courier,* Feb. 16, 1835.

11 Helen T. Catteral, ed., *Judicial Cases Concerning American Slavery and the Negro,* II, p. 279.

12 John Belton O'Neall, ed., *The Negro Law of South Carolina,* p. 11.

of bad or depraved character, or, from age or infirmity, incapable of gaining their livelihood by honest means," manumission thereafter would be legal only when a court of magistrates and freeholders had investigated the capacity of the slave to function in a free society and had endorsed the act with a deed of manumission.[13]

There is little evidence that this measure of regulation either hampered manumission or checked the growth of the free black population in any appreciable way. Large numbers of slaves continued to be manumitted according to the provisions of the act.[14] Joseph Dobbins, who had provided for the manumission of his servant Matilda through his will, found that by adding a codicil to it enjoining his executors to carry out the provisions of the act, he could accomplish his object equally effectively.[15] Some difficulty was encountered by owners who sought to emancipate minors and could not prove their ability to earn a livelihood. The legislature met the difficulty, in the case of George Bellinger of Colleton District, by stipulating that he provide for the free blacks during their minority.[16] In similar circumstances Robert Lithgow solved the problem by manumitting his twelve-year-old mulatto slave and by making the act of manumission effective nine years thereafter, during which time the slave was to be bound out as an apprentice.[17]

The legislature proved accommodating toward most petitioners against the act, and manumission by the state

[13] David J. McCord and Thomas Cooper, eds., *The Statutes At Large of South Carolina*, VII, p. 443, hereafter referred to as *Statutes At Large*.
[14] Gregorie, *History of Sumter County*, p. 132.
[15] Will of Joseph Dobbins, Record of Wills, Vol. 1, Book D, 1787–1858 (Richland County), pp. 26–27.
[16] Petition of George Bellinger of Colleton District, n.d., in Petitions Relating to Slavery.
[17] Emancipation of Jim, a mulatto slave, Miscellaneous Records, Book B, p. 621.

was not uncommon. In 1817 James Chestnut, a planter of Camden District, received $1,100 compensation from the state when the legislature emancipated his slave Scipio.[18] Although manumission was subject to a certain degree of control, there is no indication that the policy of the state was directed against it.

This twenty-year period of laxity was brought to an abrupt halt in 1820 when manumission came under the provisions of a major law regulating the activities of free blacks.[19] The Act of 1820 was clearly designed to put a brake on the increase in the free colored population. Thus while it declared that no slave might be emancipated save by an act of the legislature, the same piece of legislation also prohibited the immigration of free blacks and restricted their egress and ingress.[20] Legislative control of manumission acquires a greater significance in the context of this network of legislation against the free black. In 1822 the legislature granted the petition of John Irving to emancipate a mulatto boy "on the condition that he shall remove him without the limits of this State within two months from this date."[21] Once removed, the free black could not, by the terms of the act, reenter the state. Manumission might therefore be sanctioned only when it facilitated the policy of the state. Even so, the prevalence of slavery in the neighboring states made such removal questionable. While in a similar petition the legislature acknowledged that "it is against the necessary policy of this

18 Emancipation of Scipio, a slave, by James Chestnut, ibid., Book C, p. 396; Certificate of Manumission of slave, Scipio, by James Chestnut, which reads: "for and in consideration of the sum of $1100 to me in hand paid by Andrew Pickens Esquire, Governor of the State of South Carolina, in conformity with the act of the legislature of the said State," in Petitions Relating to Slavery.

19 See Chapter VIII.

20 Statutes At Large, VII, pp. 459–60.

21 Petition of John Irving, 1822, in Petitions Relating to Slavery.

State, to emancipate slaves and permit them to remain in the state," instincts of Southern solidarity reminded it that "it is contrary to the sacred rule of justice to emancipate them and send them to the neighboring slave-holding states." For the time being the dilemma could be resolved "by sending . . . slaves either without the limits of the United States or to a non-slave-holding State" where they would be automatically freed, a principle the legislature was to challenge thirty years later.[22]

Legislative action appears to have been a coup de main. Owners of slaves who had intended manumitting their chattels in the future suddenly found the means barred. Thus Frederick Kohne who had contracted with his slave to free him after a period of four years and two months happened to be away on the second of July, when the contract became effective. On his return in December, he discovered that the transaction was no longer legal.[23] Many other citizens, less attentive to developments in the state, were not even aware of the passage of the law. The case of Auguste Genty is, perhaps, typical.

[H]e purchased the said Sophia as long ago as the fifteenth day of May 1808 and having then been informed that the owners of slaves under the existing laws could at any time by a compliance with certain formalities effect their emancipation, he incautiously postponed to act upon the subject from day to day, and from year to year, until he understood that an act was passed at the last session of the Legislature, which prevents his performance of an act that would be so grateful to his feelings and which the said Sophia has been anxiously expecting.[24]

---

[22] Petition of John Walker, 1825, ibid.
[23] Petition of Frederick Kohne, 1821, ibid.
[24] Petition of John Reynauld, n.d., ibid.; Petition of Auguste Genty, n.d., ibid.

Though the act was followed by a spate of petitions, they were rejected with very few exceptions. Samuel Venning's heirs were compelled to forfeit their inheritance, which was contingent upon the emancipation of his slaves.[25] David Martin, a man of considerable property, was frustrated in his attempts to emancipate two daughters who were slaves, to whom he wished to bequeath his property.[26] Most pathetic, perhaps, was the case of James Patterson, a free black carpenter of Columbia who "by diligence and saving in his profession earned a sufficient sum of money to purchase his wife named Sally and his son George" for $1,000, "a sum far beyond their value."[27] Patterson's sanguinity outlasted his luck. Petitioning in 1828, and again in 1838, the free black was informed that "nothing has been offered to show that the wife and children of the petitioner (the persons most concerned in the subject of this petition) have any claims whatsoever to the interposition of the Legislature in their behalf."[28]

Even in cases where the petitioner was able to prove the black's capacity to maintain himself, the legislature was uncooperative. In such instances it was quick to point out the "crime, idleness and suffering with which *experience* has proved a state of freedom is attended."[29] Even when a black "proved his worth" in exceptional circumstances and qualified for manumission by traditional standards, he still did not meet the requisites for freedom. In 1834, a grand jury commended a slave who had heroically extinguished a fire in Sumter District. The legislature responded with

[25] Petition of the Heirs of Samuel Venning, n.d., ibid.

[26] Petition of David Martin of Barnwell District, 1827, ibid.

[27] Petitions of James Patterson, a free Negro, 1828, 1838, ibid.

[28] Report of the Committee on the Colored Population, Dec. 11, 1838, in Reports of Committees of the South Carolina Legislature.

[29] Report of the Committee to Whom was referred the Petitions of William N. Mitchell, William B. Farr, and John Ryan, for emancipation of slaves, Dec. 6, 1823, ibid.

a reward of $100; emancipation was not even considered.[30]

Faced with this impasse, owners of slaves devised every conceivable means of circumventing the law. The most common provision they made was for emigration from the state. In 1837, Mary Anthony willed the emancipation of her slaves "as soon as the laws of this State will permit. . . ." Foreseeing that such an eventuality was very remote, however, she also provided for the sale and distribution of her property among her slaves, "giving to each servant who may desire to emigrate from this state one equal share thereof, together with such testimonials or documents as may assure to him or her the enjoyment of freedom and full emancipation in any other state or country."[31] Large numbers of blacks were able to remain in the state, however, and operate as de facto free blacks by the rather clever device of trusteeship. By this means a slave was sold to a trustee who held the black in nominal servitude and administered his property for him. The will of Justus Hartman, a German immigrant, provided for this in very explicit terms.

I also give and bequeath unto the aforesaid Reverend John Bachman and John Siegling my Mulatto Slave named Peggy with her three children viz Philip, Margaret and Selestina, together with their future issue and increase upon this special trust and confidence that they will allow and permit the said Peggy and her three children with their future issue and increase to enjoy all the rights and privileges of free persons of color and should they wish at any time to depart from this State, I empower the said Trustees to furnish them with the necessary papers Chargeable to my Estate.[32]

[30] Grand Jury Presentment for Sumter District, November Term, 1834.
[31] Will of Mary Anthony, Record of Wills, Vol. 41, Book B, 1834–39 (Charleston County), pp. 864–67.
[32] Will of Justus Hartman, ibid., Vol. 42, Book A, 1839–45 (Charleston County), pp. 24–25.

William Ellison, a wealthy free black of Sumter District, found that the only way he could insure the freedom of his daughter was to have her sold to a trusted friend. A deed of trust made out to Col. William M'Creight in 1830 explicitly stated the object of the transaction to be effective emancipation, wherein "for the further consideration of one cent to me paid" Maria Ellison was "bargained, sold and delivered."[33] The terms of the trust, however, were carefully stipulated. Maria was to live with her father, who was to be free to emancipate her at any future date, within the state or elsewhere. At his death the deed was to be performed by M'Creight, who would have no claim to her services at any time.[34]

Free blacks often collaborated with one another to effect the emancipation of a wife, child or friend. To this extent racial solidarity transcended divisions of class. Richard Holloway, a wealthy free black and member of the brown elite, assumed the obligation of holding Charles Benford as his property, in order that Benford might enjoy a larger measure of freedom.[35] In 1823, James Marsh, a free black, registered a curious deed in the office of the secretary of state. By the terms of the deed, Abigail Hopton, a mulatto slave, was sold for five dollars to Robert Howard on the express condition that her time and labor were not to be subject to his control. The slave was, however, required to pay a dollar, annually, to her owner "in trust for the sole and separate use of Mary Coch, a free mulatto."[36] The relationship between either of these women and the contracting parties is not revealed in the document, but a measure

---

[33] Deed of Trust, from William Ellison, a free Negro, to William M'Creight, 1830, Miscellaneous Records, Book G, pp. 231–33.

[34] Ibid.

[35] The Holloway Scrapbook.

[36] Miscellaneous Records of the Secretary of State's Office, Book ZZZZ, 1823–25, pp. 258–59, in the South Carolina Archives Department.

of mutual aid was obviously derived from the transaction.

The problem of endowing the illegally manumitted slave was overcome by the same device. Since the de facto free black was legally a slave, he could not hold property. But both owner and slave were acquainted with the possibilities of trusteeship. The white members of a family in Columbia were able to retain its property within the natural family by this means.[37] The success of this extralegal procedure extended the already prominent group of quasi slaves, whose economic independence made them virtually free. As a petition to the legislature put it in 1840, "money is power, and none need live in servitude who can command it."[38] Such attempts to circumvent the law did not escape notice, but it was difficult to check the extralegal device, and this nominal servitude operated even more strongly than the existence of the free black to subvert the institution of slavery.

Nevertheless, circumventions of the law carried a risk for the de facto free black too. The state of quasi freedom could be enjoyed only as long as the trustee was willing to fulfill his obligations. If the trust was violated, the black had no recourse to the law. Neither a slave nor a free black, the de facto free black was subject to seizure by any white on the death of the nominal owner. His was therefore a precarious freedom and perhaps all the more precious in its want of security.

The harsh circumstances produced by legislation were mitigated somewhat by the role of the courts in interpret-

---

[37] Will of John S. Lott, Record of Wills, Vol. 3, Book L, 1787–1853 (Richland County), pp. 1–2. This property, a "house and lot containing one acre near the State House in Columbia," continued to be held by the descendants of Anne Lott, Lott's natural daughter, until 1900, when it was sold for an extremely high price. Interview with Leonardo di Andrea, genealogist, South Carolina Archives Department, June 23, 1965.

[38] Petitions Relating to Slavery (1840).

ing the law. The free status of the black would ultimately be determined by the courts, if the black sued for his freedom through his guardian, or, as was more frequent, white owners claimed possession of their property. Court decisions in this period seem clearly to have been at variance with legislative policy. In 1832, in *State* v. *Harden,* Justice O'Neall ruled that "Proof that a negro has been suffered to live in a community for years as a free man would prima facie establish the fact of freedom," recalling a decision made in 1797, when there was no legislative regulation.[39] The attitude of the courts was more realistic than that of the legislature, as the decision in *Linam* v. *Johnson* reveals. Bill Brock, a slave, had been transferred to a new owner by a formal bill of sale, after which he operated as a free black to the extent of finding himself a guardian. In 1824 the owner sued the guardian in an action of trover. It transpired in the evidence that "Bill had ever since the sale, dealt and trafficked as a free man; that he was regarded as such in the neighborhood from that time; and had been enrolled as a pioneer in the militia: That the land on which he lived was known by the name of Bill Brock's place, although it belonged to the plaintiff; and that Bill had to all appearances, cultivated it for his own benefit . . . that Bill had been permitted to hire his time and work for himself . . . that he was industrious and provident and had accumulated money . . . and it appeared that . . . he had paid the poll tax levied on free persons of color." The jury found for the defendant and the decision was upheld in appeal by Justice William Johnson on the grounds that "Bill . . . was . . . a slave, without an owner, and cast upon society as a derelict. . . ."[40]

[39] Catteral, ed., *Judicial Cases Concerning Slavery,* II, p. 350.
[40] Ibid., p. 344.

Perhaps most significant in its implications for the de facto free black was Justice William Harper's decision in *Monk* v. *Jenkins*, which confirmed the illegally manumitted slave's right to property. Upholding the act of manumission of a female slave, the judge declared: "There can be no slave without a master, and it follows that after such irregular emancipation, until seizure is actually made, the emancipated slave must stand on the footing of any other free negro."[41] The manumitted slave would, by implication, enjoy the rights of a free black. In these terms "Her legal representative has the same standing in Court that the representative of any other free negro would have."[42]

Such judicial decisions, and more particularly the decision rendered in *Carmille* v. *Carmille*, provoked the legislature to action.[43] The Act of 1841 closed all loopholes to emancipation. Entitled "An Act to *Prevent* the emancipation of Slaves," it declared void all trusts "intended to take effect after the death of the owner whereby the removal of any slave without the limits of the State, is secured or intended, with a view to the emancipation of such slave."[44]

Evidently the legislature was still open to petition, however, for memorials continued to be received thereafter. In 1853 the legislature rejected the petition of a free black, William Jackson, to manumit his wife and children, because they could "perceive no peculiar feature in the case

[41] *James W. Monk* v. *Eliza M. Jenkins,* Court of Appeals, Decrees in Equity Cases, 1832–35.

[42] Ibid.

[43] In this case, a deed of trust effected by John Carmille, following legislative rejection of a petition to emancipate his natural children, was declared void in the lower courts. The decision was reversed in appeal and provoked a strong reaction. Petition of John Carmille, n.d., in Petitions Relating to Slavery; Catteral, ed., *Judicial Cases Concerning Slavery,* II, pp. 382–83.

[44] Italics are mine. Statutes at Large Folio No. 154; *Statutes At Large,* **XI**, p. 154.

referred which would authorize a deviation from that established policy."[45] By definition, exceptions would admit exemptions from the act, but in the absence of any willingness to define the exception all petitions inevitably failed.

Nor did the courts provide any relief thereafter. In the later years of the antebellum period, judges were more inclined to condemn the decisions which had subverted legislative policy. Thus in *Broughton* v. *Telfer* (1853) Chancellor George W. Dargan challenged the decision recorded in *Carmille* v. *Carmille:* "It is founded upon what I conceive to be a very erroneous construction of the Act of 1820. . . . The decision is not in harmony with the spirit, the policy, or even the language of the Act."[46]

The Act of 1841 effectively halted the flow of manumissions, and there is little evidence of manumission by will or trust thereafter, save in cases of private extralegal agreements. One such case was the will of Francis Mishaw, a free black, who bequeathed "the colored woman Sally who was purchased by me" and her children to his executors. No mention is made of a trust, but his omission in dividing up either the family or his property among the three executors (all wealthy white men of considerable social prestige) indicates that they were to act together as guardians for the family.[47] Since the slaves were specifically *willed* to his executors, Mishaw insured his family against seizure for violation of the Act of 1841.

The act represented the culmination of a steady progression of policy which to some extent coincided with the

---

[45] Petition of Priscilla Jessup, 1845, in Petitions Relating to Slavery; Petition of William Jackson, a free man of color, 1853, ibid.

[46] Catteral, ed., *Judicial Cases Concerning Slavery*, II, pp. 393, 398, 407, 409, 427.

[47] Will of Francis Mishaw Record of Wills, Vol. 44, Book A, 1845–51 (Charleston County), p. 451.

which in turn became a more restricted and more exclusive group. The bridge by which the slave might graduate to free status had been effectively destroyed. When universal emancipation restored that bridge in 1863, the already free black lost his separate identity in the mass exodus from slavery.

changes in the growth of the free blac
tween 1790 and 1800, a period when mai.
regulated, the free colored population a.
showing an increase of 76.84 percent. Betw.
1820, the free black population increased but s.
the percentage of increase actually declined. V.
Act of 1800 may have reduced the rate of manur.
the corresponding decline in population growth wa.
very significant. The year 1820, on the other hand, con.
tutes a watershed. The free black population increased b.
only a little over a thousand in the decade from 1820 to
1830, as measured against the increase of 2,272 recorded
from 1810 to 1820. It would seem then that the law of 1820
cut off the major sources of growth in the free black community. Figures for the period 1830–60 show hardly any
increase. Between 1830 and 1840 only 355 persons were
added to the population, and the percentage of increase
fell from 16.04 to 4.48, the lowest rate in the antebellum
period. After 1841, manumission became a rather rare
phenomenon. In 1850, of a total of 1,467 manumissions in
the United States, South Carolina's freed slaves numbered
a mere two.[49]

The increase in the population of free blacks after 1840
came completely from within the free black community,

[48] Year	Free Black Population	Increase	Increase Percent
1790	1,801	—	—
1800	3,185	1,384	76.84
1810	4,554	1,369	42.98
1820	6,826	2,272	49.89
1830	7,921	1,095	16.04
1840	8,276	355	4.48
1850	8,960	684	8.26
1860	9,914	954	10.64

Federal Bureau of the Census

[49] J. D. B. De Bow, ed., *Compendium of the Seventh Census of the United States*, p. 64.

CHAPTER III

Denizens of the State

THE TERM "NEGRO CITIZEN" WAS A MISNOMER IN ANTE-bellum America, for in no part of the United States did the black enjoy a status of equality with the white. Among the free states of the North, in Massachusetts, New Hampshire, Vermont and Maine alone did the free black possess the legal right to vote. The combined colored population of these states constituted a mere 7 percent of the total Northern black population. Even here, the law provided no guarantee for the exercise of voting rights. As a Northerner explained to Alexis de Tocqueville in 1831, "The law with us is nothing if it is not supported by public opinion."[1] What Jacksonian democracy gave to "the common man" it took away from the black. In 1821 the "Reform" Convention of the state of New York practically disfranchised him at the same time that it extended the privilege of voting to all adult white males. In 1837 Pennsylvania followed suit, making no concession to propertied blacks who had previously exercised the vote.[2] The black populations of both states

[1] George Wilson Pierson, ed., *Tocqueville and Beaumont in America,* p. 514.
[2] Leon F. Litwack, *North of Slavery,* pp. 82–86.

were the largest in the North and provide an index to the black's position in Northern society.

Restrictions in many other avenues of life bear out the inferior "citizenship" of the Northern black. His testimony was not accepted in cases involving white citizens in Ohio, Illinois, Indiana, Iowa and California. Black jurors were unheard of in the North until 1860, when two were appointed in Worcester, Massachusetts—a rare phenomenon even in the temple of abolitionism.[3] In Oregon, blacks were prohibited from making contracts or holding real estate and were even denied the legal capacity to sue. When the statute books failed to delineate the black's separate and unequal status, social institutions, mob action and the widespread practice of racial segregation made the separation effective. Citizenship for the black was not acceptable to white Northerners. At the same time, the alternative of slavery was disavowed. The dilemma appears to have been resolved by a definition of that state of "in-between" into which the black was pushed. In the words of United States Attorney General Hugh S. Legaré, a prominent South Carolinian, blacks were neither "aliens" nor "citizens"; yet they "enjoy universally . . . the rights of denizens."[4]

The peculiar institution made the position of Southern free blacks even more complex. The fear of slave uprisings, ever present in the South, engendered an atmosphere of tension and suspicion, and the free black inevitably became the scapegoat for the South's prevailing insecurity by the mere association of race. Yet, in the earliest decades of this period, the free colored population was afforded many of the privileges of white citizens. In Maryland and

[3] Ibid., pp. 93–94.
[4] *Official Opinions of the Attorneys General of the United States,* IV, pp. 147–48.

North Carolina blacks were allowed to vote (in the latter
state, until 1831); they could hold property in land and
slaves in most of the Southern states; and their social institutions approximated those of the whites, although
they remained separate and not wholly equal. The gravest
restrictions the Southern free black suffered were those
which fell on his Northern counterpart with equal severity—segregation in public institutions, inequality before
the courts, the lack of opportunity for an equal education,
and social ostracism. Northern blacks enjoyed one outstanding advantage in that they could organize to pursue
their rights as free men. Security measures attending the
institution of slavery made for a very different situation
in the South. Moreover, in the decades after 1830, succes-
sive restrictions on the free black tended increasingly to
restrain the area of his freedom until the line between
slavery and freedom came to be symbolized by a pass-
number strung around the freeman's neck.

If the states were erratic in their treatment of the free
black, the federal government did not provide a satisfactory guideline. The Constitution of the United States
merely declared that "The Citizens of each State shall be
entitled to all Privileges and Immunities of Citizens in
the several States," leaving the definition of citizenship to
the individual state.[5] The issue was not confronted until
1858, when the Dred Scott decision defined citizenship in
terms that are very revealing. Ruling that, the laws and
conditions in the several states notwithstanding, black
citizenship was a question of federal policy, Chief Justice
Roger Taney looked to the Constitution to determine the
status of the black. He concluded that blacks "are not included, and were not intended to be included, under the
word 'citizens' in the Constitution, and can therefore

[5] *Constitution of the United States of America*, Art. IV, Sec. 2.

claim none of the rights and privileges which that instrument provides and secures to citizens of the United States." Carrying the argument further, the chief justice laid down what amounted to a federal prohibition of black citizenship in the several states when he declared that no state could by its own action introduce into the federal political community persons "who were not intended to be embraced in this new political family, which the Constitution brought into existence, but were intended to be excluded from it."[6] By the terms of the decision, then, the states were in duty bound to maintain the denizenship of the free black. Allowing for a certain degree of nonchalance toward federal rulings, it may be supposed that the Southern states accepted the decision without demurral on the time-honored premise that even the devil can quote scripture!

The status of denizenship was particularly acceptable to South Carolina, which, like most Southern states, wrestled with the anomaly deriving from its peculiar institution. The Palmetto State was a trifle intractable on the score of black citizenship. Where even the strongest Negrophobes in North Carolina acknowledged that "the free Negro is a *citizen of necessity*," South Carolinians admitted no such thing.[7] They did, however, address themselves repeatedly to the problem of definition, and if they found that their free blacks "have not like the freed men of Rome or Athens, become incorporated in the body politic," they sought to give their anomalous denizens a meaningful definition in the absence of meaningful rights.[8] In 1832, the courts decided that "Free Negroes without any of the political rights that belong to a citizen are still,

[6] *Dred Scott* v. *Sanford*, 19 Howard 419–22.

[7] John Hope Franklin, *The Free Negro in North Carolina*, p. 58.

[8] Helen T. Catterall, ed., *Judicial Cases Concerning American Slavery and the Negro*, II, p. 334.

to some extent, regarded by the law as possessing both natural and civil rights. The rights of liberty, life and property belong to them and must be protected by the community in which they are suffered to live."[9]

This distinction between citizen and denizen was invariably determined on the basis of color. In South Carolina, the word "mulatto" held more than the usual connotations of racial hybridism because a mulatto, by virtue of his black admixture, was not entitled to the rights of a citizen; or, as Chief Justice Hugh Rutledge held in an action for slander, "the words were in themselves actionable . . . because if true, the party would be deprived of civil rights."[10] It was not unusual for citizens to be relegated to denizenship overnight; skeletons in the cupboard had a curious propensity for airing themselves in the local courtroom.[11] The line of division was a very tenuous one, however; for light-skinned mulattoes had a stronger chance of acquiring citizenship than darker-skinned quadroons or octoroons. Whenever a person's claim to citizenship was questioned, it was color, rather than the degree of admixture, which prevailed. The courts upheld this dubious distinction for want of more satisfactory criteria. In 1826 Justice William Harper explicitly declared color to be the basis for the definition of civil status: "It [denizenship] has no doubt been the result of the mark which nature has put upon them. For where this has been obliterated, some have obtained, and now enjoy all the rights of citizens; some who have lost that distinctive mark, hold offices, as well as lands, and even seats in the legislature. . . ."[12] To all intents and purposes, the free black remained a denizen as long as his

[9] Ibid., p. 350.
[10] Ibid., p. 307.
[11] See Chapter I.
[12] Catteral, ed., *Judicial Cases*, II, pp. 334–35.

skin betrayed his origin; when he became light enough
he graduated to citizenship.

The free black's conception of his own status varied
with the degree of laxity afforded him by Southern society.
In the first flush of independence, the victory of the slogan
"no taxation without representation" seems to have inspired South Carolina's free blacks to press for the amelioration of their own position. In 1791, a memorial of
Thomas Cole, bricklayer, and P. B. Mathews and Mathew
Webb, butchers, "on behalf of themselves and other Free-
Men of Color," declared that although they had been
enumerated as citizens of South Carolina in the apportion-
ment of Representatives for the state in Congress, they
were subject to many disabilities by the old law of 1740
and placed on the same footing as slaves. The petition
continues:

Your Memorialists shew that they have at all times since the
Independence of the United States contributed and do now
contribute to the support of the Government by chearfully
paying their Taxes proportionable to the Property with others
who have been during such period, and are now in full enjoyment of the Rights and Immunities of Citizens and Inhabitants of a Free Independent State.

That as your Memorialists have been and are considered as
Free-Citizens of this State they hope to be treated as such, they
are ready and willing to subscribe to such Oath of Allegiance
to the States as shall be prescribed by this Honourable
House. . . .[13]

Having presented their case for treatment as free citizens,
however, the petitioners showed some confusion as to what
this status might really imply. They hastened to assure the

[13] Memorial of Thomas Cole, P. B. Mathews and Mathew Webb, in
Petitions Relating to Slavery.

legislature that they did not "presume to hope that they shall be put on an equal footing with the Free white citizens of the State in general" and addressed themselves, rather, to specific grievances, such as their inability to give testimony against a white man.[14] But behind the facade of subordination and the disavowal of any claim to equality a strong resentment is evident against the anomaly, which, if it baffled eminent jurists in the state, must have been surely less comprehensible to the ill-educated but rational free black.

This early assertion of citizenship evoked a strong and unfavorable response among the white people of Charleston. Not long after, rumors of subversive activity among the blacks led to the rifling of Mathews' home, and the petitioner found it necessary to issue a public denial of his role in the anticipated "plot."[15] This was the last recorded attempt of free blacks to demand a more satisfactory definition of their status. As regulations grew progressively severer in the nineteenth century, the free black submitted more and more to his environment. Looking back during Reconstruction, even so affluent a former free black as William Holloway marveled at the revolution the Civil War had brought about in status and in dignity.[16]

The most fundamental right to which the free black was legally entitled was that of liberty. By the court's admission, even insofar as the free black was a denizen, the state held an obligation to protect him in the enjoyment of his right to liberty in his person. Yet the definition of this freedom contained a curious ambiguity. For the black, liberty was not an inalienable right. Even if his title to

[14] Ibid.
[15] *City Gazette and Daily Advertiser* (Charleston), Sept. 7, 1793.
[16] George B. Tindall, *South Carolina Negroes*, pp. 140–41.

freedom derived from his birth, it was liable to forfeiture as the state saw fit. In December 1860, the South Carolina House of Representatives debated a piece of legislation intriguingly entitled "A Bill to provide for the temporary sale of vicious and vagrant free persons of color." Reporting on the bill, the Committee on the Colored Population did not question the principle involved but declared that "whilst they approve of the policy of selling into slavery such of that class of free Persons of color as have *forfeited* their claim to our support and protection, [they] object to some of the provisions of the Bill referred. . . . but propose a Bill which in their judgment will more effectively carry out the object arrived at."[17] The war which broke out the following year killed the legislative proposal, but the attempt is singularly revealing of the ambiguities attending the rights of denizenship.

The denizen was also required at all times to be able to prove his status. When a black was legally manumitted, a copy of the deed was delivered to him which he had to carry on his person at all times. All free blacks, whether manumitted or freeborn, were required to possess certificates of freedom.[18] Failure to produce such a certificate when challenged by any white citizen would justify a black's seizure as a slave, for as Justice William Harper admitted in *Monk* v. *Jenkins,* "the presumption of our law is against a Negro's freedom." [19] Loopholes in the law led to innumerable instances of kidnapping and subsequent enslavement. In such cases, the black was rarely able to retrieve his freedom, for judicial procedure prohibited the testimony of black against white at the same time that

17 Report of the Committee on the Colored Population, Dec. 8, 1860, in Reports of Committees of the South Carolina Legislature.
18 See Appendix D.
19 *James W. Monk* v. *Eliza M. Jenkins,* Court of Appeals, Decrees in Equity Cases, 1832–35.

it imposed the burden of proof on the plaintiff.[20] If the black was lucky, some white man, acting as his guardian, would sue on his behalf. The number of such suits for ravishment of ward was phenomenal. Many of them involved cases of fraud, where minors were enticed away or trusting candidates for manpower were promised work and dealt bondage.[21] One particular intriguing case reveals the extent to which ignorant free blacks were at the mercy of unscrupulous officials. In this case, a constable of the Charleston police fabricated a charge against two free blacks, who were subsequently committed to jail. Here they were kept, until they consented to indenture themselves to a friend of the constable, who claimed he would befriend them by defraying the expenses of the case against them. That was the last heard or seen of the free blacks. When the state tried the constable for fraud in the discharge of his duties, the defendant "acknowledged that he did the act, for the purpose of making money of them, and exulted that he was in no danger, as they had been sent off, where their complaints could not be heard, supposing that their presence was indispensably necessary to his conviction."[22]

Such frauds seem to have been rife in South Carolina, for in 1816 the usually unfriendly grand jury of Charleston decried "the show of lawful proceedings, which has been fictitiously given by some persons to the horrible practice of inducing free negroes in jail or in debt to bind themselves for a trifling sum for several years and by a transfer of the indenture and a chain of inhuman proceedings cause them to be sold into the interior or out of the

[20] *Statutes At Large*, VII, p. 398.

[21] Catteral, ed., *Judicial Cases*, II, pp. 308, 319–20, 307, 379, 388–89; Petition of J. E. Holmes on behalf of Negro, Catherine, in Petitions Relating to Slavery.

[22] Catteral, ed., *Judicial Cases*, II, p. 304.

state."[23] In 1820, legislative action imposed a penalty on the sale of free blacks, but the measure seems to have been ineffective, for in 1822 the legislature once more debated the need for a bill to prevent the kidnapping of free blacks. The debated measure finally became law in 1837.[24]

The sale of free blacks by the state, on the other hand, was lawful and not uncommon. Until 1821, free blacks found guilty of harboring fugitive slaves were liable to public sale if they were unable to pay the fine imposed on them.[25] Free black tax defaulters were also subject to temporary enslavement until the required sum was earned, while white citizens who defaulted suffered a fine or imprisonment.[26] Liberty for the black was therefore hedged about by a multiplicity of qualifications. It was a right enjoyed only on sufferance and, as such, maintained only by a combination of vigilance, subordination and sheer good luck.

The growing importance in the South of a capitalistic economy guaranteed to the free black the sacred and inviolable right of private property. The South's refusal to brook any interference with the institution of slavery derived, in large part, from her positive defense of the sanctity of ownership.[27] Inasmuch as free blacks contributed to the system through their efforts in agricultural and commercial activity, the dominant society extended to them the privileges basic to the promotion of capitalist enterprise. Of all the Southern states, free blacks were prohibited from holding property in Georgia alone, where

[23] Grand Jury Presentment of Charleston District, Spring Term, 1816.
[24] *Charleston Mercury,* Dec. 19, 1822; *Statutes At Large,* VI, p. 574.
[25] The Act of 1821 replaced the penalty with "corporal punishment not extending to life or limb." *Statutes At Large,* VII, pp. 460–61.
[26] See Appendix E.
[27] See George Fitzhugh, *Sociology for the South, or the Failure of Free Society.* See also Richard N. Current, "John C. Calhoun, Philosopher of Reaction."

the free colored population was comparatively negligible. South Carolina's free blacks were unhampered in the enjoyment of property rights, and in the city of Charleston, where opportunities for capitalist enterprise were greatest, they throve in a variety of fields ranging from artisanship to speculation in real estate. Thus they held a positive advantage over competing urban slaves, who could own no property.[28]

The free black's right to private property was enhanced by the right to contract and the access afforded him to the state's laws of insolvency. Free persons of color were permitted to make affidavits on matters involving collateral even in the superior courts and could take the oath under the Insolvent Debtor's or Prison Bounds Act.[29] The denizen's role in the economic life of the state was recognized and encouraged. Justice Daniel E. Huger held in 1823 that "The act of 1788, for establishing the bounds of the prisons . . . does not exclude free persons of color: nor would it be just, after forcing them into Court, to withhold a privilege so important [the right to take the oath under the Insolvent Debtor's Act], and which is granted to all others."[30] Free blacks exercising this right, moreover, were afforded the facilities necessary for maintaining such an action. Thus Primus Swain, in custody on a writ of *capias ad satisfaciendum,* was able to make a schedule of his estate on oath to satisfy his creditors, and the city court arranged for the settlement of the action which would secure his liberation.[31]

Unlike the slave, the free black possessed the right to his own labor. He could chose his occupation, work his own

[28] Petition of Myra Reid, a Free Person of Color, for Confirmation of Title, in Petitions Relating to Slavery.

[29] John Belton O'Neall, *The Negro Law of South Carolina,* p. 14.

[30] Catteral, ed., *Judicial Cases Concerning Slavery,* II, p. 324.

[31] *Charleston Mercury,* Dec. 17, 1822.

hours (if he was economically independent), and live where he chose. He also enjoyed some meaningful social rights such as those of marriage and the family, except when his spouse was a slave. Free blacks were afforded considerable freedom of movement within the state, but they ran the risk of seizure in areas unfamiliar to them; since this practice was rather common, it operated as a restraint on free movement. Until 1822, however, free blacks were allowed to leave the state and reenter it freely.[32] Legislation following the Vesey trials prohibited the reentry of free blacks on pain of imprisonment and provided for enslavement for the second offense. The law was retroactive and many free blacks who had already left the state found themselves in exile.[33] While the measure was intended to restrict the free black's communication with the outside world, no corresponding restrictions were imposed on his movement within the state, save in Charleston, where, after 1822, the free black was required to register twice a year with the intendant, record his birthplace and date of entry into the state, and if absent for any period of time explain where he had been.[34]

Although excluded from the regular judicial system,

[32] One of the suspects in the Vesey trials first heard of the attempted insurrection while in New York; he returned shortly after, only to be incriminated in the plot himself. Statement of Prince Graham, Document B, Documents Relating to the Vesey Uprising.

[33] Most noteworthy among them was Jehu Jones, a wealthy and well-respected free black, who left the state at the invitation of the American Colonization Society in New York. Subsequently abandoned by the society, Jones repeatedly petitioned the legislature for permission to return and appears to have succeeded, for his burial is recorded in the Register of St. Philip's Church. However, his daughter was arrested and imprisoned for violation of the law of 1822 but was later pardoned by the governor, at the solicitation of some of Charleston's most prominent citizens. Petitions of Jehu Jones, Petition of Ann Deas, in Miscellaneous Records; Pardon of Ann Deas, ibid., Book J, p. 317.

[34] A Digest of the Ordinances of the City Council of Charleston From the Year 1783 to October 1844, p. 22.

the free black was allowed some of the legal rights accruing to citizens. All free blacks (save those included in the terms of the Negro Seamen's Act of 1822) were entitled to the right of habeas corpus.[35] Free persons of color were also legally recognized in the capacity of *sui juris,* i.e., in the right to sue.[36] In practice, however, this right was interpreted and misinterpreted so freely that it seems to have produced confusion in the minds of plaintiff, counsel and judge alike. When the issue was finally decided it was held that the black could sue only through his guardian, which, in effect, denied his legal capacity. Definitions of his concomitant right to give evidence and prove his case added even more confusion. In 1839, in *Chartran v. Schmidt,* Justice B. J. Earle decided that "It would be a gross injustice to allow a free person of color to bring an action and withhold the means of making it effectual,"[37] but his opinion proved the exception rather than the rule.[38] In a very unusual decision it was held that the mulatto issue of a white woman might testify in court;[39] the decision provoked a storm of protest in judicial circles, and succeeding judges never tired of orating on the obvious misinterpretation of the law.[40] It was eventually decided in the federal courts that free blacks "could not by the laws of South Carolina be examined as witnesses" even on behalf of a white man.[41]

Whether blacks possessed the right to petition, which they sometimes exercised, was even more dubious. Since no legal ruling was available, the existence of this right depended largely on the mood of the legislature, to whom

[35] John Belton O'Neall, ed., *The Negro Law of South Carolina.*
[36] Ibid., p. 13.
[37] Catteral, ed., *Judicial Cases Concerning Slavery,* II, p. 372.
[38] Ibid., pp. 319, 344, 295.
[39] *State* v. *M'Dowell,* ibid., p. 289.
[40] Ibid., p. 339.
[41] Ibid., pp. 461–62.

the petitions were addressed. In 1817, the Charleston delegation in the House of Representatives, reporting on a petition by free persons of color to establish a church in Mt. Zion, conceded "That although they were doubtful of the political right of the petitioners to address the Legislature, yet as the petition was couched in humble and respectful terms, they gave it much serious consideration. . . ."[42] Recognition of the petition varied also with the reputation of its author. When Ephraim Wilson, a relatively obscure denizen, petitioned for the remittance of his title to a plot of land, the legislature implicitly recognized his right to petition in granting the plea. But when Amos Cruikshanks, a free black from Charleston, known for his role in the establishment of an independent black church and suspected of complicity in the Vesey uprising, petitioned the legislature through a member of the House, a Mr. Dunkin, the issue became one of principle. As the *Charleston Mercury* records, "an objection was made against receiving a petition from a free man of color and after some debate, it was thrown out."[43] Thus, in the absence of an impartial ruling on the issue, recognition of the right to petition became purely subjective. When, a year before the outbreak of the Civil War, Elizabeth Jane Berg, a free black, prayed for permission to become a slave, the legislature decided that, in this case, the petition was worthy as a model, and a bill might be drawn up to "provide for all cases of this kind."[44]

In their role of denizens, free blacks between the ages of eighteen and forty-five were required to perform "fatigue

[42] Petition of Sundry Free Persons of Color to Establish a Church in Mt. Zion, 1817, in Petitions Relating to Slavery.

[43] Petition of Ephraim Wilson, ibid.; *Charleston Mercury*, Dec. 7, 1822.

[44] Report of the Committee on the Colored Population on the Petition of E. J. Berg, a Free Person of Color, in Reports of the Committees of the South Carolina Legislature.

work" and militia duty, though in the latter instance they functioned as musicians in a company rather than as active soldiers. They were entitled to the same pay and subject to the same rules as the white militia,[45] however, and free blacks who had served in the Revolutionary War were entitled to regular payment and a war pension.[46] Black participation in the militia was welcomed in times of war, but white citizens had some misgivings about the feasibility of such participation in times of peace. Ever mindful of the threat of slave uprisings, citizens of Kershaw District, for instance, pointed to the danger of activity which "would enable them to witness and become acquainted with the use of arms and the evolutions of war . . . that, Martial Music, and the warlike movement of troops are calculated to fire there bosoms with feelings, which, at an evil hour, may burst forth with distructive fury and destroy the peace and lives of our fellow citizens."[47] Evidently the state was more impressed with the wisdom of enlisting free blacks on the side of law and order, however, for the provisions for black service in the militia remained on the statute books even through the Civil War.

The welfare of the denizen concerned the state as much as that of the white citizen and his property, the slave. When John Packer claimed remuneration for the care of a poor free black woman, the legislature reimbursed him on the implicit recognition that this was, after all, the state's responsibility.[48] Although specific provisions for poor free blacks were late in being legislated, records of the Charles-

[45] *The Militia and Patrol Laws of South Carolina*, pp. 28, 37.

[46] Petition of John Featherston, Documents Relating to "Negroes in the Defense," No. 2,567, in manuscripts of the South Carolina Archives Department; Revolutionary War Pension No. R 2,160.

[47] Petition of Sundry Citizens of Kershaw District, 1828, in Petitions Relating to Slavery. Misspellings appear in the original.

[48] Petition of John Packer, ibid.

ton poorhouse reveal that many free persons of color found refuge there.[49] In 1855 two white doctors in Charleston set up a hospital for blacks, charging a nominal fee of two dollars a week for nursing and board.[50] The gesture appears to have had the desired effect, for two years later the city of Charleston passed an ordinance for the support of disabled free blacks and set aside a section of the poor house for the city's free colored population.[51] Lunatic free blacks presented a graver problem, for, unlike the slaves, "their state of unrestrained freedom to roam when they may and where they may" made them a danger to society. The legislature repeatedly debated whether to build an asylum for blacks, to be financed partly by owners and guardians, but at the outbreak of the Civil War the measure had not passed.[52] The state's tardiness in the performance of its obligations was more a reflection of interest than of principle, however, and the free black's civic right to facilities provided by the state was unchallenged.

To a considerable degree, then, free blacks enjoyed legal rights that were denied the slave population. However, the insecurity deriving from the existence of slavery drew them within the orbit of restrictive police regulations which developed around that institution. Directly the most restrictive of these measures was South Carolina's infamous patrol system, which was almost as long established in the state as the institution of slavery and which had remained untouched by reform for a span of two centuries.[53] The patrol was essentially a military corps, re-

[49] See Appendix C.
[50] Richard C. Wade, *Slavery in the Cities; the South, 1820–1860,* p. 139.
[51] *Ordinances of the City of Charleston,* p. 46.
[52] Report of the Committee on the Colored Population, Dec. 14, 1847, in Grand Jury Presentments, 1790–1865.
[53] Howell Meadows Henry, *Police Control of the Slave in South Carolina,* pp. 29–44.

cruited compulsorily from the citizenry. By the provisions instituting it, patrolmen could invade the homes of blacks in a search for firearms and could administer a maximum of twenty lashes to any black found away from home without a pass between sunset and sunrise. The system demanded not merely submission but a measure of servility from free blacks, whose free movement constituted a threat by example. Refusal to stand when arrested or "obstinacy at trial" would cost the free black a fine of forty dollars.[54] More severe, however, was the free black's constant subjection to arrest, interrogation and corporal punishment by stray patrolmen, whose frequent disorderly conduct provoked repeated protests even from white citizens.[55] So repressive was the system of surveillance developed through the patrol system that a Northern visitor to the slave states stood aghast at this curious manifestation of white paternalism.

But go to the bottom of this security and dependence and you come to police machinery such as you never find in towns under free government; citadels, sentries, passports, grapeshotted cannon, and daily whippings for accidental infractions of police ceremonies. I happened myself to see more direct expression of tyranny in a single day and night at Charleston, than at Naples (under Bomba) in a week.[56]

Subjected to the police regulations of slavery, the free black was tried before the "slave courts" and included in the terms of the slave code established in 1740. According to its provisions, blacks were denied the right to self-defense against a white, and black testimony against a

---

[54] Ibid., p. 47.

[55] Ibid., *passim*.

[56] Frederick Law Olmsted, *The Cotton Kingdom: A Traveller's Observations on Cotton and Slavery in the American Slave States,* I, p. 350.

white man was inadmissible in the courts. Until 1821, the death penalty did not apply to a white man who murdered a black.[57] Blacks convicted of non-capital crimes were dealt a distinct set of penalties, ranging from mutilation, whipping, and confinement in the stocks to imprisonment. The definition of capital crimes was broader in the case of the black. As Justice O'Neall expounded the state laws: "There are . . . cases in which the slave or free negro . . . *from his status,* would be guilty of a higher crime than a white person would be, under the same circumstances."[58]

The trials of blacks were conducted by a court composed of two magistrates and five freeholders. According to the letter of the law, the system was designed to provide for a crude form of trial by jury, for the prisoner was entitled to select the five freeholders from among eight summoned by the magistrate.[59] In practice, the prisoner had little recourse to legal concessions, for arrests and trials were often dispensed with in twenty-four hours, the defendant hardly having time to consider the charge against him. Miscarriages of justice were frequent; not only were the freeholders ignorant of the law, but popular prejudice and excitement also often dictated the verdict in a case involving a capital crime.[60] It was widely recognized that judicial procedure relating to blacks was, in the words of Justice O'Neall, "the worst system that could be devised." Although governors and grand juries repeatedly inveighed against the system, reform was limited

[57] *City Gazette* (Charleston), Dec. 11, 27, 1821.
[58] O'Neall, *Negro Law,* p. 28.
[59] Ibid., p. 33.
[60] Grand Jury Presentments of Laurens District, Spring Term, 1858; Newberry District, Spring Term, 1859; Abbeville District, Fall Term, 1859; Reports of the Committee on the Colored Population, 1839, 1858, in Grand Jury Presentments, 1790–1865.

to a single law in 1833 which granted slaves and free blacks convicted of a capital offense the right of appeal to a circuit court.[61]

The free black lacked the protection afforded the slave, whereby the slave's master might intervene on his behalf.[62] The law required all free persons of color to have guardians, but even where this requirement was fulfilled, the guardian was inevitably less interested than the slaveholder, to whom the conviction of a slave would mean the loss of valuable property. To all intents and purposes, he was an intermediary between the free black and society, underwriting the latter against abuse of freedom by the former while guaranteeing the black his free status. His role, however, was less that of a protector than that of a guarantor. That such was the interpretation generally given to his functions is evident in the numerous petitions to the legislature demanding that free blacks conduct their business only in the name of a guardian, or that guardians be responsible for the debts of free persons of color.[63] The guardian assumed the capacity of a master without any of the obligations attending ownership of slaves. His quasi authority could be enforced, negatively, by the threat of withdrawing his guardianship.

The free black paid dearly, in cash, to maintain his freedom. Chief among the financial exactions upon him was the capitation tax of two dollars a year imposed in 1792 on free persons of color between the ages of sixteen and fifty. The act did not discriminate between wage

[61] Henry, *Police Control of the Slave*, pp. 59–64; O'Neall, *Negro Law*, p. 35; *Statutes At Large*, VI, 489–90.

[62] The law provided, for instance, that if a slave died in jail due to ill-treatment, the jailor was responsible to the master and would be required to pay him the full value of the slave. *Statutes At Large*, VII, p. 362.

[63] Grand Jury Presentments of Lancaster District, Fall Term, 1849; Marion District, Spring Term, 1852; Union District, Spring Term, 1852.

earners and dependents, and the exaction operated most harshly on free black women, who petitioned frequently "that not only from the natural imbecillity and incapacity of themselves but also from abject poverty and other causes, it is not in their power to subsist themselves."[64] In addition, the state's numerous assessments on its white citizens fell also on the free black, and the capitation tax sometimes exceeded these impositions as well. The following tax schedule is that of a middle-class free black and may be considered average.[65]

St. Philip's and St. Michael's (general parish tax)	$24.25
Road tax	.24
Cross road tax	
Public building tax	1.21
Free schools tax	7.28
Total	$32.98

While this total does not include the capitation tax, it does indicate the heavy burden of taxation on free blacks, many of whom barely earned as much as the total amount they were required to pay. A petition presented by twenty-three free blacks of Camden a year after the tax schedule went into effect eloquently expresses the weight of financial oppression. The petitioners complained that they were

a Poor needy people; have frequently large Families to maintain; and find it exceedingly difficult and distressing to support the same and answer the large demands of the Publick; which

---

[64] Petition of Sundry Females of Color in Richland District, 1806, in Petitions Relating to Slavery; Petition of Sundry Citizens of Sumter District, 1830, ibid.; Petition of Sundry Citizens of Richland District, n.d., ibid.

[65] Receipt of General Tax From Margaret Noisette, Noisette Papers.

appears to them considerably more than double what was formerly Exacted from them; In consequence of which they conceive their Situation in life but a small remove from Slavery.[66]

In many cases the act did indeed result in a form of temporary slavery, for blacks failing to make returns or to pay the double tax subsequently imposed on them were sold at public auction for a specified period of time, during which they earned the required sum.[67] The free black had no insurance against fraud on the part of tax collectors, and in one instance thirty-one free blacks nearly lost their freedom when the sheriff of Charleston connived with the tax collector at misappropriating the city's funds.[68]

The city of Charleston, in particular, seems to have conceived of its denizens as a bottomless fund. When the city council set up a municipal guard in 1822 in the wake of the Vesey trials, the expenses involved were defrayed by taxes imposed on free black tenants and landlords, with a further tax of ten dollars on all free blacks who participated in any "Mechanick trade within the limits."[69] The prevailing attitude appears to have been informed by the rationalization that, if the state had to suffer its denizens, it may as well exact the maximum from them.

The distinction between denizen and citizen was continually emphasized by a series of social inhibitions imposed by law, chiefly with a view to maintaining the

[66] Petition of Free Negroes of Camden District, 1792, in Petitions Relating to Slavery.

[67] Catteral, ed., *Judicial Cases Concerning Slavery*, II, p. 356; Petition of Joseph Mickle, in Miscellaneous Records. See also Appendix E.

[68] William Edward Hayne, Comptroller General, to Maj. Benjamin Hart, Jan. 30, 1840, in manuscripts of the South Carolina Archives Department.

[69] Petition of Sundry Persons of Color and Guardians for Return of Tax Paid for Municipal Guards, in Petitions Relating to Slavery.

subordination of the black race. For although the free black might be granted legal concessions appropriate to denizenship, the element of race imposed a predetermined ceiling on such concessions and made necessary the absolute differentiation of denizen and citizen. This differentiation is perhaps best symbolized in the deference required of the free black toward the white man. No black, slave or free, could strike a white, whether in self-defense or otherwise. This intrusion of law into social relationships must have been bewildering and rather irksome to the general mass of white citizens, who were unfamiliar with the complexities of the institution of slavery. The state records contain, for instance, a curious memorial from George Wheathers, a white petitioning for the release of his black assailant. The assault apparently occurred while both were in a state of intoxication, and the petitioner pleaded that the free black had suffered punishment far in excess of his crime.[70] The lash was even more a symbol of the black's degradation. When exasperated citizens of Clarendon District demanded that white men guilty of retailing liquor to slaves be subjected to the lash, the legislature threw up its hands in horror. Whipping, it declared, was a chastisement associated with the colored race. Not only would the white culprit lose caste, but the spectacle of a white man subjected to this humiliation would inevitably excite instincts of insubordination among the black population.[71]

The black's subordination was further ensured by supervision of his general deportment. In the best traditions of Southern decorum, Charleston's free blacks were prohibited from "whooping or hallooing anywhere in the

[70] Petition of William Bryant to John L. Wilson, Governor of South Carolina, and affidavit of George Wheathers, ibid.
[71] Report of the Committee on the Colored Population, May 1846, in Grand Jury Presentments, 1790–1865.

city, or of making a clamorous noise, or of singing aloud any indecent song," of "speaking aloud any blasphemous or indecent words, or crying out in a blasphemous, obscene or indecent manner," or of making "any loud or offensive conversations" at street corners. There was to be no "dancing or other merriment" without prior permission from the city wardens.[72] But decorum surely yielded to deference when free blacks were forbidden to smoke a pipe or cigar or carry a cane in public, on the pain of twenty lashes and forfeiture of the pipe or cane to any white person who seized it from him.[73] The free black did not perhaps conform to the Sambo image, but he was expected at all times to follow rather closely in Sambo's shadow.

Subtle forms of social discrimination often tended to make regulatory measures more effective. An incipient pattern of racial segregation separated white and colored parks, reserved the East Battery and the South Battery for the exclusive occupancy of whites, and required that white and colored laborers repairing roads work on different sides.[74] When a victim of theft advertised a reward for the detection of the culprit, the free black's remuneration invariably amounted to only a fraction of what was offered the white man.[75] Strenuous efforts were made to restrain free intercourse between black and white, particularly among hoi polloi, where such intercourse was most common. This was perhaps the strongest impulsion behind the numerous petitions against grogshop owners, "habitual promoters of sedition, who, by reason of their occupation

[72] *Digest of City Ordinances, 1783–1844,* pp. 170, 173, 174–75.
[73] Ibid., p. 173.
[74] Grand Jury Presentment of Lexington District, Fall Term, 1841; Report of the Committee on the Colored Population, Dec. 2, 1841, in Grand Jury Presentments, 1790–1865.
[75] *Charleston Mercury,* Jan. 11, 25, 1822.

should lose caste in the community . . . by bringing the negro . . . in such familiar contact with the white man. . . ."[76] Miscegenation invariably drew the wrath of race-conscious citizens, more so because this was an area of freedom that neither church nor state could control. An outraged grand jury of Edgefield District proposed that all mulattoes born of white women should be sold at public auction, a measure it hoped would constitute "a remedy for the wrongs of the South."[77]

The free black was, in many respects, the scapegoat for the state's racial dilemma. Whatever civil status he was accorded was inextricably linked with the institution of slavery and with the fact that, though not a slave, he was still a member of the subordinate race. In this context, the legal definition of black denizenship is apt to be misleading. The free black undoubtedly enjoyed some civil rights which accrued to him by virtue of his free status. His enjoyment of natural rights, however, is highly questionable. There was no right the black enjoyed that was not defined as forfeitable. His life, his liberty, indeed his very presence in the state were subject to the whims and vagaries of the state legislature and to the willingness of white citizens to tolerate an anomaly in their society. By contrast, the growing stability of democratic institutions guaranteed more than ever to the white population the natural rights of "life, liberty and the pursuit of happiness." The hiatus between denizenship and citizenship was very real, if not absolute. Graduation from the one to the other was possible only when the black could change the color of his skin.

[76] Grand Jury Presentment of Charleston District, Fall Term, 1847, Spring Term, 1851.
[77] Grand Jury Presentment of Edgefield District, Fall Term, 1859.

CHAPTER IV

A World in Shadow

THE FREE BLACK LIVED ON THE MARGIN BETWEEN TWO societies, the slave and the white, and in this anomalous position he experienced what W. E. B. Du Bois called a "double-consciousness."[1] For, although a free man operating in a society whose norms were set by the dominant white race, he was identified racially with the slave population. To this extent, he constituted a classic example of what sociologists have termed "the marginal man."[2] The free colored population experienced both a conflict with and an assimilation of two cultures, though to a lesser extent than most marginal types, for the transplanted African slave was invariably subjected to an abrupt process of Americanization. In very broad terms, it might be said that within the context of the slave system in the South the free black belonged culturally to the dominant group but racially to the subordinate group.

[1] W. E. B. Du Bois, *The Souls of Black Folk*, p. 3.

[2] The term was originally used by Robert E. Park in "Human Migration and the Marginal Man," 892. A detailed study of the "marginal man" appears in Everett V. Stonequist, *The Marginal Man*. Stonequist, who deals largely with racial and cultural hybrids, analyzes the behavior of such types as the Anglo-Indian in India, the Jew in Europe and the mulatto in the United States and draws a general pattern of behavior from the varied responses to circumstances of marginality.

The marginal man, as defined by Everett V. Stonequist, arises from a bicultural or multicultural situation.

The natural desire . . . is to advance toward the group occupying the higher status. He may be forced to accept the status of the lower group, possibly becoming their leader. He may be rejected by both groups. Where accommodation, rather than conflict, prevails, . . . [the marginal group] may constitute a middle class. . . .[3]

In these terms, three options were available to the free black: identification with the white group, assimilation with the black, and, in the event of social isolation or bicultural assimilation, the development of a separate class or community. This chapter will examine the response to these options on the part of South Carolina's free blacks. It must be noted at the outset that free blacks did not constitute a homogeneous group, drawn as they were from different walks of life and subjected as they were to different economic pressures. However, a general pattern of behavior is discernible from the evidence available; where necessary, the pattern has been tempered by the variable.

The source of the free black's marginality was undoubtedly the institution of slavery. His inferior civil status derived largely from the fact that vast numbers of his race were recognized as property, rather than as persons, and were therefore beyond the pale of civil rights.[4] Significant numbers among the free colored population had once been slaves; even among the freeborn the daily contact with slaves, regular public auctions and whippings, and the frequent irritations of the patrol system all served as a constant reminder of the peculiar circumstances in

[3] Everett V. Stonequist, "The Problem of the Marginal Man."
[4] See Chapter III.

which they operated as "free persons of color" rather than as "free citizens."

Yet the free black's attitude toward slavery was rather ambiguous. Freed slaves making their way up in the world often considered the acquisition of their own slaves a sound investment, and many a black fortune was founded on slave labor.[5] Free blacks bargained and sold their slaves to one another, often at a profit. While some transactions were intended to insure the security of a favored house slave, others were the response to a greater pecuniary motive. Thomas Bonneau, founder of a school for free blacks, stipulated in his will, for instance, that if two girls—slaves—were to "prove obstreperous," he "would rather that they be parted with by being put in hands of or sold to Kentucky merchants—in that case the money will be sure."[6]

At the same time, however, even larger numbers of free blacks connived at undermining the institution of slavery. Free black homes were often the refuge of fugitive slaves, particularly in the city of Charleston, where the presence of a vast throng of blacks, slave and free, hampered the detection of runaways. Evidently such activity was directed against the institution of slavery per se, rather than against the white owner. One such case found "a Justice of the Peace and two freeholders . . . about to try a free person of color for harboring a slave, belonging to Amy Le Prier, another person of color."[7] However, some measure of racial solidarity appears to have informed

[5] Will of Cyrus Page, Record of Wills, Vol. 16, Book A, 1774–79 (Charleston County); Will of Hannibal Dearington, ibid., Vol. 28, Book A, 1800–07 (Charleston County), pp. 3–4; Will of William Ellison, ibid., Vol. 2, Book 14 (Fairfield County), pp. 14–15.

[6] Will of Thomas Bonneau, ibid., Vol. 39, Book C, 1826–34 (Charleston County), pp. 905–7.

[7] Helen T. Catteral, ed., *Judicial Cases Concerning American Slavery and the Negro,* II, p. 320.

the actions of those opposing the peculiar institution. Members of the Brown Fellowship Society who expelled a fellow member, George Logan, in 1817 for having "held a conspiracy and caused said Robinson, a free black man to be sold as a slave," were themselves slaveholders.[8] Men like Morris Brown who frequently bought and manumitted slaves were acutely conscious of the position of their race and sought, in every way, to instill a sense of dignity and self-respect into the degraded mass of blacks.[9]

The free black's social intercourse was largely confined to the slave population. In rural areas free blacks had no other choice because they were too few and too widely scattered, and free black intermarriages with slaves were most common in these areas. At the same time urban centers such as Charleston brought the free black into close contact with the slave. At the lower levels particularly, little social distinction was made between the free black and the urban slave—they conducted the same kinds of trade, congregated in the same taverns and attended the same churches. Since many urban slaves were permitted to live away from their owners, there developed whole areas of settlement where slave and free black lived side by side. Charleston Neck, in the northern part of the city, was such a ghetto, where free blacks and slaves mixed freely and enjoyed the benefits of close communal living. The

[8] Theodore D. Jervey, *Robert Y. Hayne and His Times*, pp. 68–69.

[9] Foster Burnet to Morris Brown, Bill of Sale of a Negro Man Slave Named London, Nov. 18, 1813, in Miscellaneous Records; Certificate of Manumission of Slave London, Nov. 19, 1813, ibid. Morris Brown later founded the African Methodist Episcopal church in Charleston. On his expulsion from the state in 1822 he migrated to Philadelphia, where he continued to be active in the affairs of the A.M.E. Church, becoming a bishop in 1828. Himself a man of little education, Brown firmly believed in the need to educate the black as the first step toward challenging the preconceptions of black inferiority. [Daniel A. Payne?], *The History of the African Methodist Episcopal Church.*

free black was accorded a slight social distinction in that he was his own master, but this superiority was not always acknowledged. The domestic slave, reared in the genteel traditions of upper-class white society, did not contain his scorn for the upstart "free nigger."[10] There had developed, even among the slaves, positive caste distinctions paralleling the divisions in white society, and the free black had no place in this rigid hierarchy.

Yet, on another level, the free black wielded a well-defined superiority over the slave. Where free blacks owned slaves, a distinct master-servant relationship was maintained. The common bond of race did not serve in any way to mitigate the severity of bondage. William Ellison of Sumter District, a freed slave who had over a hundred slaves working for him by 1860, was renowned for more than his material prosperity; his frequent advertisements for runaway slaves gave him something of a reputation in the district.[11] A French traveler in 1790 described another affluent free black with some understatement: "The severity excepted, with which this emancipated slave treats his negroes, his conduct is said to be regular and good."[12]

The relationship between the free black and the white population was far more complex. The techniques of police control and the deference required by law defined the free black population as a subordinate group. Yet, the law notwithstanding, there was a considerable degree of social intercourse between the free black and the white.

[10] Howell Meadows Henry, *Police Control of the Slave in South Carolina*, p. 182.

[11] T. S. Sumter, *Stateburg and Its People*, p. 32; Anne King Gregorie, *History of Sumter County*, p. 135.

[12] Francois, Alexander du Frederic, Duke de la Rouchefoucault-Liancourt, *Travels Through the United States of America, the Country of the Iroquois, and Upper Canada in the Years 1795, 1796, and 1797*, p. 602.

Most obvious, of course, was the practice of intermarriage. Despite repeated petitions, overt hostility and the attaching social stigma, whites of both sexes continued to intermarry with free persons of color.[13] Both parties were frequently drawn from the middle and upper middle classes and the free blacks passed into white society without much ado. Pindaim, an emancipated slave in the parish of St. Paul's, Charleston, married a white woman and later gave his mulatto daughter in marriage to a white man.[14] Both of William Ellison's daughters married white men; one of them was welcomed by her father-in-law, a Baptist minister who lived on a farm adjoining Ellison's and who left his estate to the children by the marriage.[15]

Extralegal alliances were, of course, far more common. White men frequently had colored mistresses whom they maintained and provided for in their wills.[16] Social restrictions often prevented open marriages between white women and free black men, resulting in some clandestine alliances. One case is of particular interest. "Mrs. Sarah Jones, a white lady" was the mistress of a free black, Joe Rogers, who had abandoned his legitimate family and who eventually left his estate to his mistress. Their illegitimate son, however, recognized his free black half sister and left her a considerable share of his estate. The illegitimate

---

[13] Petition of Sundry Citizens of Barnwell District Praying Further Legislation in Reference to the Colored Population, n.d., in Petitions Relating to Slavery.

[14] La Rouchefoucault-Liancourt, *Travels*, p. 602.

[15] Ellison's son Reuben married a slave, much to his father's displeasure. Gregorie, *History of Sumter County*, p. 135; Will of William Ellison, Record of Wills, Vol. 2, Book 14 (Fairfield County), pp. 14–15; Will of Rev. Samuel Whorter Yongue, ibid., Book 13 (Fairfield County), pp. 50–51; Will of Rebecca Yongue, ibid., Vol. 3, Book 19 (Fairfield County), pp. 503–5.

[16] Will of Justine, a free black, ibid., Vol. 32, Book E (Charleston County), p. 831; Catteral, ed., *Judicial Cases Concerning Slavery*, II, pp. 326–27.

branch of the family eventually passed as white, while the legitimate branch continued to be classed as free persons of color.[17]

Association among free blacks and whites of the upper class was by no means rare, undoubtedly because the latter were secure socially. Daniel Payne recalled that, as a free black in Charleston in the 1830s, he had been able to develop a friendship of perfect equality with the family of Dr. John Bachman, the South Carolina naturalist.[18] Charleston's most prominent citizens patronized the hotel of Jehu Jones, a free black, knew his family well and befriended them in times of trouble.[19] The Noisette family continued to maintain a close friendship with the executors of the will of their ancestor, the Frenchman, Philippe Stanislaus Noisette. The executors, "having a desire to keep up the name of Noisette in a respectable position for future years," managed the Noisettes' estates for them and undertook to cover the wild oats of many a young Noisette.[20] There was undoubtedly an element of paternalism in these relationships, but when affluent whites had equally affluent free black neighbors who maintained every symbol of upper-middle-class status, that paternalism was hard to maintain. Coming Street in Charleston, for instance, was the residence of Dr. Elias Horlbeck, a white physician, and four wealthy free blacks, one of whom, William McKinley, was by far the wealthiest of all five

[17] Will of Joe Rogers, Record of Wills, Vol. 39, Book C, 1826–34 (Charleston County), pp. 1,168–71; Will of Jacob Rogers, ibid., Vol. 42, Book A, 1839–45 (Charleston County); *Fifth Federal Census*. I am indebted to Mr. Harold Delorme, genealogist, Columbia, S.C., for providing this and many other cases of free blacks who crossed the color line.

[18] Daniel A. Payne, *Recollections of Seventy Years*, p. 24.

[19] Petetion of John L. Wilson for Jehu Jones, 1823, in Petitions Relating to Slavery; Petition of William Lance for Jehu Jones, 1827, ibid.

[20] John Siegling to Dr. Elias Horlbeck, Charleston, Jan. 24, 1859, Noisette Papers.

residents.[21] More direct evidence of acceptance in white
society is recorded in the diary of Richmond Kinloch, a
wealthy millwright, who lived among Charleston's crème
de la crème and was wont to spend his "retreats" with
them.[22]

These relationships apply, of course, to the upper
echelons of free black and white society. An inter-
mingling of a different sort took place among hoi polloi
in the marketplace, the taverns, the gambling dens and
the brothels.[23] Here, unhampered by social conventions
and considerations of caste and status, a truer fraternity
existed between black and white. The lower-class free
black did not need to carve a niche for himself in white
society: he was merely a confrere in a fellowship of have-
nots.

Within the free black group in South Carolina were
strong divisions of class, modeled on the divisions in white
society but not as well-defined. Antebellum white society
was broadly divided into upper, middle and lower classes:
the planter and old merchant families constituted the
upper class; the professionals and slightly parvenu land
speculators and merchants the middle class; and the artisans, small farmers and unskilled laborers the lower class.
The upper class among South Carolina's free blacks
closely approximated its white counterpart, but its bound-
aries were somewhat broader. Included were the large

[21] E. Horace Fitchett, "The Free Negro in Charleston, South Carolina"
(Ph.D. diss., University of Chicago, 1950), p. 54.

[22] Diary of Richmond Kinloch.

[23] Affidavit Concerning a Negro Dance in Charleston, 1795, in Petitions
Relating to Slavery. The witness, a member of the Volunteer Patrol, testified that he saw "a white man jump out of the Balcony, and a Negro fellow out of a Window two story high," but he was less concerned with the
separate and daring exits of the revellers than with the fact that white
and colored should presume to mix in a house recently occupied by a
white man.

landowners, wealthy merchants and real estate speculators, who were also well established in a trade. Among the upper class were the Holloways, whose carpenter's establishment, handed down from generation to generation, was supplemented by heavy investments in land; the Kinlochs, wealthy millwrights who also owned plantations; the family of William Ellison of Sumter District, whose patent for a cotton gin supplemented a thriving plantation; Thomas Small, carpenter and real-estate speculator; and Jehu Jones, Charleston's best-known hotelier, who also had title to many valuable sites on Broad Street, the city's business center.

At the bottom of the social ladder were the free black artisans, yeoman farmers and the large mass of unskilled laborers in the city. The artisan group was perhaps the most varied, ranging from the independent craftsman who maintained his own modest establishment to the skilled worker who was employed by a white or free black craftsman. Some free black artisans were in better material circumstances than others, but they all were relatively uneducated, lived in the same areas and had no real status in society. The yeomanry was chiefly composed of subsistence farmers, usually owning between ten and thirty acres of land which they supplemented by their skilled labor as carpenters, blacksmiths and rafthands.[24] The mass of unskilled free black laborers was hard put to compete with slaves "hiring their time" in the cities; many resorted to vagrancy and crime and some evolved a convenient migrant cycle from almshouse to workhouse to jailhouse.[25]

A notable deviation from the white pattern was the absence of a recognizable middle class, due, in large part,

[24] See Chapter V.
[25] Petition of Joseph Mickle, 1829, in Miscellaneous Records; Records of the Poor House.

to the want of professionals among free blacks. There were little or no opportunities for education and training in professional skills, and with the exception of two school-teachers, Thomas Bonneau and William McKinley—both wealthy landowners whose schools were more philan-thropic than directly educational in purpose—no free blacks were listed for long in any of the professions.[26] The nearest approximation to a middle class might be found among the more prosperous artisans who were sometimes able to acquire property through their savings. Examples of this group were Sam and Sally Bugg, of whom we are told, "Both were industrious, and the surplus of their gains, after paying expenses, was employed by Sam in the purchase of some property."[27] But the distinction of small property-holding was insufficient to remove an individual from one class to another, particularly when the hiatus between the two existing groups was so wide. Social mobility was virtually nonexistent within the free black group. The upper class had developed its wealth and posi-tion over four or five generations, during a period when restrictions on free blacks were less stringent and op-portunity was greater. The rising artisan of the early nineteenth century had no viable social status to aspire to; he merely hovered on the upper fringes of the lower class, a man in the crowd but not of it.

In these circumstances, class divisions were supplanted by caste distinctions, closely approximating the existing pattern of white society. Among the upper-class free blacks, social gradations were as rigid as the distinctions which in white society separated the Porchers and the Ravenals from the Guignards and the Taylors, and the Guignards

26 The professional class in New Orleans provides a contrast of some interest. In 1850, the census listed one architect, sixty-one clerks, four doc-tors, five jewellers, twelve teachers, and one music teacher. Fitchett, "Free Negro in Charleston," pp. 69–70.

27 Catteral, ed., *Judicial Cases Concerning Slavery*, II, p. 380.

and the Taylors from the Calhouns and the Wilsons. Families like the Kinlochs, the Mitchells, the Holloways and the Dereefs formed an elite and set the pace, as it were, in free black society. In turn, they closely followed the pattern of ingroup behavior among the white elite. Their choice of partners in marriage, of sponsors for the baptisms of their children and of executors for their wills was invariably made from the small group of free black first families.[28] To a considerable extent, their commercial transactions reveal a tendency to keep their property within the families thus related by marriage. They had their own social organizations, literary associations and library societies, which were as exclusive as the white social groups in Charleston. Outstanding among these was the Brown Fellowship Society, founded in 1790. Membership was confined to lighter-skinned "free brown men" and their descendants; a maximum of fifty members was always maintained; and while members met every month in social concourse, a tradition of strict decorum was prescribed and maintained at all meetings. The society had its own burial ground and its own school, both of which were strictly reserved for members and their families.[29] Following the pattern set by the Brown Fellowship Society, similar organizations were established by other groups among free blacks of the upper class, representing free black social gradations. Notable were the Humane Brotherhood (originally the Society of Free Dark Men) and the Unity and Friendship Society.[30]

To a considerable degree, gradations of caste cor-

[28] Diary of Richmond Kinloch; Will of Richmond Kinloch, Record of Wills, Vol. 46, Book A, 1851–56 (Charleston County), p. 46; Will of Thomas Bonneau, ibid., Vol. 39, Book C, 1826–34 (Charleston County), pp. 905–7; The Holloway Scrapbook.

[29] Jervey, *Hayne and His Times*, p. 434; Holloway Scrapbook.

[30] James B. Browning, "The Beginnings of Insurance Enterprise among Negroes"; Jervey, *Hayne and His Times*, p. 6.

responded to gradations of color. Where the dominant race was white, values associated with a light skin became the dominant values. Moreover, positive advantages might be derived from a light skin, as light-skinned mulattoes discovered in their relations with the white race. It was not uncommon for light-skinned Afro-Americans to cross the color line into white society.[31] Furthermore, the mulatto offspring of miscegenation were often provided for by their white fathers and thus held a material advantage over the pure black. Francis Louis Cardozo, natural son of a Jewish businessman, obtained a college education in Glasgow, Scotland; the children of Philippe Stanislaus Noisette inherited his extensive farm in Charleston; and Ann Lott fell heir to a piece of land adjoining the state capitol in Columbia, the value of which appreciated rapidly as the city developed.[32] Light-skinned Afro-Americans might fraternize with white men less conspicuously than dark-skinned Afro-Americans; for this reason they were more acceptable in white society. The subtle distinctions which centered around complexion intruded even into the intimate relationship between husband and wife. We are told of Abigail Jones and Eliza Lee, the wives of two well-known hoteliers who were wont to hobnob with their white patrons: "Both women were mulattoes, cleverer than their dark husbands, and so oppressed them. . . ."[33] More overtly, the free black social organizations discriminated between the brown and the black. Membership in the Brown Fellowship was limited to "free brown men." The Friendly Moralist Society was even more explicit:

[31] Catteral, ed., *Judicial Cases Concerning Slavery*, II, pp. 359, 386.

[32] William J. Simmons, *Men of Mark*, pp. 428–30; Noisette Papers; Will of John Lott, Record of Wills, Vol. 3, Book L, 1787–1853 (Richland District), pp. 1–2; Schedules I and II, Unpublished Agricultural Schedules of the Seventh Census.

[33] Mrs. St. Julien Ravenal, *Charleston, the Place and the People*, p. 461.

"Should it be charged and proven that any member is not a *bona fide* brown man, he shall be fined $2.00."[34] It was in response to this discrimination that Thomas Small founded the Society of Free Dark Men, which later changed its name to the Humane Brotherhood.[35] Within the free black group, therefore, there were divisions which were rooted in its marginal circumstances and which provided a poor foundation for the growth of a community.

The social institutions which developed among the free black group approximated, at all levels, those established in white society. Unlike the slave, whose every sphere of life was controlled by his master, free blacks were able, to a large extent, to order their own lives. The institutions of marriage and the family were highly developed among them, as was also the principle of inheritance. A trade might be handed down from generation to generation, the eldest son in the family usually inheriting the business from his father.[36] A remarkable case in point is the late Mr. Robert Ingliss, who died in Charleston in 1957, the last of seven generations of barbers.[37] Traditional antebellum social values such as piety, education and a good marriage were as firmly rooted in the free black community as they were in white society. In these terms, if the free black group was not an integral part of antebellum Southern society it constituted an adjunct.

Upper-class free blacks in particular appear to have developed all the accouterments of high society. Among the bequests made to her husband and children by Susannah Cart, a wealthy free black, was a pew in St.

[34] Browning, "Insurance among Negroes," p. 424.

[35] Jervey, *Hayne and His Times*, p. 6; interview with Mrs. Anna Patrick and the late Miss Ella Small, Charleston, July 16, 1965.

[36] Holloway Scrapbook.

[37] Interview with Mrs. Irene Noisette and Mrs. Naomi Brown, Charleston, July 15, 1965.

Paul's Church and a chaise, both symbols of status in the upper echelons of white society.[38] Richmond Kinloch's estate included, besides his real estate and slaves, a "patent lever silver watch made by Roskell of Liverpool," a silver pencil case and a collection of books that might have been seen in the library of any genteel Charlestonian.[39] Formal dinners, debutante parties, traditions of courtship and other niceties of etiquette where rigidly observed by upper-class free blacks.[40] Membership in the Brown Fellowship Society was as much a symbol of social prestige to a black as membership in the St. George Society was to a white.

Social intercourse between free blacks and whites remained the exception rather than the rule and was usually limited to the upper classes. The growing white middle class, whose political influence was in the ascendant, strongly resented the free black and consistently underscored his subordinate status through legislation.[41] Middle-class planters in the backcountry regarded free blacks of the lower orders as a constant threat to the security of the slave system, and hostility toward the free black was strongest in rural areas.[42] In the city, genteel, affluent free blacks presented a challenge to the rising middle class: recognition of their achievements would be suicidal, and still less was there an inclination to leave the door of opportunity open to the rising black artisan. The outcome was a denial of social status to the free black; in

[38] Will of Susannah Cart, Record of Wills, Vol. 36, Book C, 1818–26 (Charleston County), pp. 984–85.

[39] Will of Richmond Kinloch, ibid., Vol. 46, Book A, 1851–56 (Charleston County), p. 46.

[40] Holloway Scrapbook.

[41] Petition of the South Carolina Association, 1822, in Petitions Relating to Slavery; see also Chapter VIII.

[42] Petitions Relating to Slavery. A remarkable circumstance in the Vesey trials was the degree of confidence that well-established Charleston planters like the Bennetts and the Prioleaus continued to place in their accused slaves. Document A, Documents Relating to the Vesey Uprising.

these circumstances he was isolated socially. He could not assimilate with the slave population because his institutions, his social norms, his entire way of life, in effect, were geared to the dominant white society; nor was he recognized by that white society toward which he constantly aspired.

Acceptance in white society did not follow the free blacks approximation of that society. The extent to which the free black recognized the social isolation to which he was condemned cannot be clearly defined. There is some evidence, however, of the elite's self-conscious attempt to reach the lower orders of free blacks and to build an organic community within the marginal group. Alongside the numerous exclusive social organizations emanating from the upper levels of free black society and informed to some extent by the concept of noblesse oblige which prevailed in white society were a number of charitable institutions. The Minors' Moralist Society, established in 1803 by reputable free blacks like Richard Holloway, James Mitchell and Thomas Bonneau, was designed to maintain and educate free colored orphans. During its short lifespan (it was defunct by 1847) it provided for many an indigent free black child.[43] Another such organization was the Christian Benevolent Society organized in 1839 "to relieve the necessities of the poor as far as their means will allow."[44]

The social organizations of upper-class free blacks also represented an attempt to develop some measure of social security within the particular society, independent of either the white patron or the state. The Brown Fellowship Society provided for the widows and orphans of deceased members and guaranteed an education to mem-

[43] Payne, *Recollections*, p. 14.
[44] Holloway Scrapbook.

bers' children. The Humane Brotherhood, approximating even more closely the white Masonic orders, on which the free blacks appear to have modeled their societies, made provision for the support of members in times of sickness, accident or death. If a member was imprisoned on any account, his family received a weekly allowance from the brotherhood.[45] These prototypes of insurance activity reveal a certain degree of self-consciousness within the free black group, and to some extent the commercial transactions of free black land speculators underscored the tendency toward mutual dependence and trust, for they tended to sell only to one another, attempting to keep the land within the group and to ensure that generations to come would be well provided for. It must be noted, however, that such activity was limited to small groups at the top of the social scale.

In spite of restrictions imposed on the education of blacks, free blacks continued to maintain schools for members of the community. These schools were too few and too short-lived to be of real importance, but the effort is noteworthy. Throughout the antebellum period individuals or small groups of students were taught by free blacks who had been able to acquire an education in an earlier period when restrictions were less severe. The students in these schools were drawn from different walks of life: children and adults, the wealthy and the small artisan. However, the better-known schools which provided a more regular education had a rather restricted clientele. A school operated for a short while by Simeon Beard was private and somewhat exclusive, and Daniel Payne's students were largely drawn from the leading white families

[45] *Rules and Regulations of the Brown Fellowship Society;* Holloway Scrapbook; Browning, "Insurance among Negroes," p. 424.

in Charleston.[46] Besides the school maintained by the Brown Fellowship Society for its members, the only other school of note was that of Thomas Bonneau, which was large enough to require two assistants and functioned from 1803 to 1829.[47] The students in both the latter institutions belonged, with rare exceptions, to the upper echelons of free black society.

A greater degree of fraternity appears to have existed at the religious level among some of the black congregations of the various denominations. Black members of the Baptist church in Charleston had their own "society" within which they met and worshipped and it became a beneficiary in the will of a wealthy member, Maria Creighton, who left her house as a place of worship for its members and the rest of her estate in trust to the Baptist church, "to apply it to the support of poor blacks in Charleston."[48] Similarly, wealthy free blacks who worshipped in the Congregational church on Meeting Street in Charleston established the "Euphrat Society" and built their own burial ground in 1832. One of its founding members was Thomas Small (founder also of the Society of Free Dark Men), who held the exclusive activities of light-skinned upper-class free blacks in great contempt.[49] Even so, there is no evidence that the Euphrat Society was itself open to rich and poor, dark skinned and light skinned alike. Little is known of its activities beyond the fact that it maintained a burial ground for members, as many other religious organizations did.

Of far greater significance was Morris Brown's effort to

[46] Simmons, *Men of Mark*, p. 162; Payne, *Recollections*, p. 25.
[47] Holloway Scrapbook.
[48] Will of Maria Creighton, Record of Wills, Vol. 39, Book C, 1826–34 (Charleston County), pp. 1,176–79.
[49] Register of Mesne Conveyance, C-10, pp. 430–31 (Charleston County).

establish an independent African Methodist Episcopal Church.[50] Brown's attempt was clearly designed to bridge the gap between the free black elite and the lower orders by comprising both free men and slaves. A man of considerable property, Brown was yet extremely popular and well-respected among the slaves and poorer free blacks who constituted the mass of his congregation. Had he succeeded, there might have developed the beginnings of a black community with leadership passing to the more independent and better educated free black group. Wealthy free blacks like Richard Holloway and Thomas Small had been closely attached to church activities, serving as lay preachers and class leaders among the black congregations of the white churches. Membership in a composite black church might well have drawn them beyond the periphery of the black lower orders to which their acts of charity and benevolence had taken them. In consequence, the church might have provided a sounder base for community within the free black group. But Brown's efforts were discredited by the large-scale implication of black class leaders in the Vesey affair, and his attempts at black religious unification died with his expulsion from the state.

These divergent efforts at unification did not yield a cohesive free black community, for they were rooted in divisions which could not easily be bridged. Distinctions of color and caste penetrated deeply into free black society, fissuring the group. The chasm separating the free black upper class from the lower orders, moreover, presented an almost insurmountable obstacle to the building of an organic community. With no real middle class to bridge the gap, the free black elite could barely touch the lower classes through organized acts of charity. Nor was its ef-

50 This is discussed at length in Chapters VI and VII.

fort wholehearted. The upper-class free black did not wholly identify himself with the entire free black group. His whole way of life was a close approximation of that of the dominant white society toward which he aspired. In this context the development of a separate community was not a recognizable option to him: far more viable was the option of passing into white society and losing his identity with the free black group, or, in the face of failure to pass, of developing patterns of elite behavior which would give him status within his own society.

What the free black experienced socially was a pull in two directions, though the pull toward the white society could not be resolved. The lower orders, in closer fraternity with the slaves, felt the common bond of race more strongly but were continually aware of the position of affluence that might be attained by dissociation with the slave. Members of the upper class, enjoying a superior position within their own black group, constantly reached for status within the dominant, white group, whose norms they had imbibed. The crisis of the Civil War resolved the dilemma temporarily by severing in two the black group. Propertied free blacks who had a vested interest in Southern society supported the Confederacy, for the most part, overtly or covertly, while the mass of free blacks went the way of the slave masses and in some cases served as spies for the Union armies.[51] Yet the Civil War was a moment

[51] Theodore Jervey refers to the cold civility with which Richard Dereef greeted the Reverend Henry Ward Beecher immediately after the Civil War. Beecher apparently remarked to a friend on his disappointment at such treatment by a man whose race had reason to be grateful to him, but his confidant reminded him that Dereef's hospitality had been admirable, in view of the loss of property he had suffered during the war. Theodore D. Jervey, *The Slave Trade, Slavery and Color*, pp. 220–21; Sumter, *Stateburg and Its People*, p. 32; Frank A. Rollin, *The Life and Public Services of Martin R. Delaney*, p. 198; Charles E. Cauthen, ed., *The State Records of South Carolina*, p. 61; David J. McCord and Thomas Cooper, eds., *The Statutes At Large of South Carolina*, VIII, p. 53.

of crisis, when the options were absolute and not necessarily viable. The free black's role in society achieves better focus in the context of the black community which
emerged into the postwar world.

The Emancipation Proclamation made social beings of
a vast throng of chattels. The freed black now had the
capacity to achieve social stability through institutions like
marriage, the family, private property and the church,
though, admittedly, this achievement did not occur immediately. In the actual process by which the ex-slave
developed his social institutions and began to take his
place in society, leadership was provided, for the most
part, by the well-to-do free blacks of the antebellum
period. Black legislators, state officials, teachers and newspaper editors were drawn from that corps of free blacks
whose earlier experience and education had fitted them
for the task.[52]

On the surface this would appear to be an about face
on the part of the free black, and to some extent ex-
pediency and the opportunity for leadership dictated
identification with the black masses. But in contrast with
the anomalies attending antebellum society, the free black
was now presented with a very real option. Identification
with the slave race no longer jeopardized his position nor
degraded him. He could now run for political office, supported by the mass of enfranchised ex-slaves, and take his
place in the legislature alongside the white man. As a
symbol of citizenship, this position made him equal with
the white. But his vision was no longer directed solely toward white society; it embraced also the black masses to
whom he owed his position and toward whom he had assumed an obligation. Admittedly some light-skinned

[52] George B. Tindall, *South Carolina Negroes, passim;* Joel Williamson, *After Slavery,* pp. 316–17, 366.

blacks still thought in terms of passing into white society, for values once imbibed are not easily lost. But men like Francis Louis Cardozo identified themselves with the black group, going on to become its leaders.

The opportunities for self-fulfillment available to blacks enabled them to develop that esprit de corps which had been lacking in antebellum society. The change in situation is perhaps best expressed in the words of two members of the Holloway family, black leaders before and after the war. Surveying the role of the antebellum free black, James Harrison Holloway, vice-president of the Brown Fellowship Society, made this rather incisive analysis, on the one-hundred-and-fourteenth anniversary of the society's founding:

On the one side we have the dominant race and on the other we have the backward race. The first looked with a scrutinizing eye on our every movement, so as to charge us with being a disturbing element in conditions that existed. . . . but fortunately there were the Classes in society, and as our fathers allied themselves with them, and as a consequence, they had their influence and protection; and so they had to be in accord with them and stand for what they stood for. If they stood for close fellowship, so did our Fathers. If they stood for high incentive, so did our Fathers; if they stood for education, so did our Fathers; If they stood for slavery, so did our Fathers, to a certain degree. But their sympathies were with the oppressed. . . .[53]

In contrast to those prewar attitudes, in 1883 William Holloway made an appeal to South Carolina's blacks:

. . . get homes, engage in business of a commercial character and deal with each other. The patronage of a single ward will

[53] Holloway Scrapbook.

support a store; that store will need a clerk, and maybe other assistants; these needs will give employment and put money in pockets. Don't wait to make a big beginning; start in a small way, and develop your enterprise.[54]

This change in the free black's social frame of reference is of the greatest significance. It reveals, first, that group alienation had not gone so far as to cut the free black adrift when the Civil War altered the terms of race relations. It might be said that the free black now found his roots, for the first time, in his own membership group. But even more important, a dysfunctional identification with a white reference group had given way to a more functional identification with the black's own membership group.[55] Identification with white society could only have been functional in an open social structure which provided for mobility and an actual graduation to status within that group. Such had not been the case in antebellum society. In a situation that was far more real, the free black now opted to join the ranks of his membership group. Ingroup alliances, caste divisions and discriminations of color were, of course, to continue; but the chasm between the marginal group and the membership group had been bridged for the most part. The free black had found his place in society.

[54] Quoted in Tindall, *South Carolina Negroes*, pp. 140–41.

[55] The terms "reference group" and "reference relationship" are frequently used by sociologists to describe the interaction of social groups. A reference relationship arises when an individual aspires to membership in a group other than his own and assimilates the norms of the nonmembership group. The reference group refers to the nonmembership group whose perspective becomes the point of view of the individual in question. The reference relationship is functional when the aspirations of the individual can be fulfilled, but when, as in the circumstances of the marginal man, the individual is denied access to the reference group, the relationship is dysfunctional. Robert K. Merton, *Social Theory and Social Structure*, pp. 225–28; Tamotsu Shibutani, "Reference Groups and Social Control," in Arnold M. Rose, ed., *Human Behavior and Social Processes*, pp. 128–44.

CHAPTER V

In the Markets of Freedom

THE ECONOMY OF ANTEBELLUM SOUTH CAROLINA WAS A curious hybrid of capitalism and feudalism. On the one hand, white citizens engaged in the free enterprise of an unregulated economy; on the other, the slaves, who formed the bulk of the labor force, operated within an economic system that was almost feudal. Although the slave was frequently subjected to the vagaries of the labor market, he was assured a minimum of security. His basic needs—food, clothing and shelter—were provided by his owner. His health was often the responsibility of his master, and he derived some measure of protection from the fact that his master's profits depended on his well-being.

The free black existed outside this orbit. Owing no personal obligation to a master and receiving no protection in return, his survival depended on the degree of economic independence he could maintain. To a considerable extent his economic independence was facilitated by the rights he enjoyed as a free man: he could own property, contract for his services and use his labor as he pleased. But the restrictions imposed on him by virtue of his color gave him less than complete access to the opportunity for

93

free enterprise afforded the white man. Despite these handicaps, many free blacks attained positions of security and affluence in the economic life of South Carolina. They also contributed, in a very positive way, to the wealth of the state.

South Carolina's economy was essentially agricultural, supported chiefly by a plantation system which employed slave labor. The true extent to which free blacks contributed to this economy cannot, of course, be accurately judged. Well-established Charlestonians like Thomas Bonneau and Richmond Kinloch invested their profits in plantations outside the city.[1] Free black planters, per se, who held cotton and rice plantations which were cultivated by slave labor, were exceptional cases of affluence, but the few who were able to maintain plantations competed very successfully with white planters. The Duke de la Rouchefoucault-Liancourt referred in an account of his travels in 1794 to a free black whose plantation was worked by two hundred slaves; the man, Pindaim, was so successful that he was able to breach the barriers of white society.[2] The case of William Ellison of Sumter District is perhaps the most exceptional. Freed when he was twenty-nine, ex-slave April Ellison took his master's name, realizing "that such a change although apparently unimportant would yet greatly advance his interest as a tradesman."[3] Regular savings and a patent for a cotton gin enabled him to acquire a plantation, to which he added the plantation house of Gov. Stephen D. Miller and eventually the house

[1] Will of Thomas Bonneau, Record of Wills, Vol. 39, Book C, 1826–34 (Charleston County), pp. 905–7; Will of Richmond Kinloch, ibid., Vol. 46, Book A, 1851–56 (Charleston County), p. 46.

[2] Francois, Alexander du Frederic, Duke de la Rouchefoucault-Liancourt, *Travels Through the United States of America, the Country of the Iroquois, and Upper Canada in the Years 1795, 1796, and 1797*, p. 602.

[3] Miscellaneous Records, Book D, p. 369.

of General Sumter.[4] A member of the white Episcopal church in Sumter, Ellison owned a pew in the church as well, and, on his death, he was buried in the white cemetery.[5]

The labor force on the plantations was seldom, if ever, recruited from the free black rural population because it was profitable for neither the planter nor the free black. The freeman had better opportunities for a livelihood in rural areas if he learned a trade and worked as a blacksmith, carpenter or mechanic, as most rural free blacks did. Some free blacks were listed in the census as "hirelings"; in these cases it is far more likely that they worked as laborers in trades or as servants in white homes, rather than as field hands on the plantations. The field slaves were frequently subjected to rigorous conditions of labor and the harsh discipline of the overseer. The freeman could avoid this oppression unless sheer necessity drove him to slave labor. In some very rare cases, free blacks served as overseers on plantations, though they were almost invariably mulattoes who had some connection with the planter's family. The overseer on Joseph Allston's plantation (also an Allston) was a mulatto, as was William Tann, overseer on the Murray plantation on Johns Island, who "from the fairness of his complexion was thought to be and passed for a white man."[6]

On the whole, rural free blacks maintained the same economic standards as the yeoman farmers who made up the majority of South Carolina's white population. Many free blacks were small farmers. David Grooms of Richland District was perhaps typical. Styled a "planter" in the

---

[4] T. S. Sumter, *Stateburg and Its People*, pp. 31–32; Benjamin J. Lossing, *The Pictorial Fieldbook of the Revolution*, II, p. 476.

[5] Anne King Gregorie, *History of Sumter County*, p. 135.

[6] William Jay, *Inquiry into the Character and Tendency of the American Colonization and American Anti-Slavery Societies*, p. 22.

federal census, he owned eleven acres of land valued at
$25, used machinery on his farm to the value of $5, raised
sixty bushels of Indian corn a year, and owned a mule, two
milch cows, fourteen other cattle and nine swine, all
valued at $154.[7] Yet, even among free black as among
white farmers, the acreage and value of land varied greatly,
ranging from modest subsistence farms to small plantations which required hired or slave labor. The schedule
for Abbeville District in 1850 reveals the extent of this
range. The schedule lists fourteen farmers among a total
of 357 free blacks. The majority of free blacks in the
district was composed of artisans and laborers. Many of
them, however, owned land and supplemented their earnings with the profits yielded by their farms. Ralph Burnet,
a blacksmith, owned 30 acres of land and livestock valued
at $160 and marketed two 400-pound bales of cotton an-
nually. Andrew Volantine, a "hireling," was wealthier
than the blacksmith in that his farm yielded three times
as much marketable cotton.

The economic condition of the rural free black varied
also with the area in which he resided. In cotton-growing
regions like Abbeville and Barnwell districts, production
for the market supported material prosperity. By contrast,
in the upper pine region of Richland District, subsistence
farming was common. The expansion of the city of Columbia, however, raised the value of land within the district
considerably, and free black subsistence farmers here were
as well-to-do as the small planter of either Abbeville or
Barnwell. Jesse Bolton's 22 acres in Richland were valued
at $220, for instance, while William Rouse's 102 acres in
Abbeville District were worth only $200.[8]

[7] Unpublished Agricultural Schedules of the Seventh Census (Richland
District).
[8] Ibid.

Census Schedule for Abbeville District in 1850*

Name	Acres of improved land	Acres of unimproved land	Cash value of land	Value of farming machinery	Horses	Mules	Milch cows	Other cattle	Swine	Value of livestock	Bus. of wheat	Bus. of Indian corn	Bus. of oats	Bales of cotton of 400 lbs. each
Daniel Wanslow (farmer)	150	140	1,400	400	6	1	8	10	40	920	60	540	100	10
David Furman (farmer)	55	85	250	25	4	0	8	7	15	263	0	250	60	3
Ralph Burnet (blacksmith)	50	0	——	10	3	0	3	2	12	160	0	100	20	2
David Wilson (cooper)	10	0	——	5	1	0	2	1	13	56	0	80	0	2
Andrew Volantine (hireling)	40	0	——	10	2	0	1	3	15	135	50	100	40	7
Jack Kellar	16	0	——	5	1	0	0	0	0	20	0	50	0	0
Cato Coleman (farmer)	40	69	900	10	4	0	3	5	3	260	12	120	15	5
William Marion (farmer)	20	0	——	43	1	1	1	2	4	70	5	70	20	2
Maria Strauther	10	0	——	5	1	0	3	4	8	50	0	25	0	1
Jonathan Strauther (wheelwright)	12	0	——	5	1	0	2	0	5	100	0	100	10	0
William Rouse (farmer)	60	42	200	25	3	0	1	10	4	255	0	300	10	2
Lefate W. Allen (farmer)	50	0	——	15	5	0	2	5	54	656	0	300	50	11
Anthony Green	50	0	——	100	3	1	3	4	14	?	20	50	20	3
Eliza Rouse	15	0	——	5	1	0	1	4	14	164	34	100	0	2

* Unpublished Agricultural Schedules, Seventh Federal Census, 1850. Abbeville District, South Carolina.

The following table[9] indicates the extent to which conditions varied in Abbeville, Barnwell and Richland, the three districts in which free blacks were most heavily concentrated, though they rarely amounted to even 7 percent of the total population. The table also indicates, though to a limited extent, the proportion of the contribution made by free blacks to the wealth of their districts. Their productivity was heaviest in Indian corn and livestock, which points to a subsistence economy. Free blacks owned considerable amounts of land, but their numbers were never extensive enough to yield a significant contribution to cotton, the mainstay of the state's economy. The same was true, however, of the majority of white yeoman farmers, whose farms were essentially the same as the blacks.

The yeoman farmer, however, was not typical of the rural free black. Although there was less opportunity in the country than in the city, most rural free blacks earned a livelihood as small artisans. Evidently they were usually successful in their trades, for many of them owned land and often caused local white mechanics to complain about competition from the colored population.[10] Even so, the trades they plied were somewhat restricted in comparison with those of artisans in the city. The census for Richland District reveals this distinction most clearly. In the first schedule, for Columbia and its environs, free blacks are listed as tailors, shoemakers, sawyers, carpenters, cabinetmakers and stable-keepers—many of whom owned real estate of high value. Free blacks listed for the rest of the district, in Schedule II, were predominantly "planters" (that is, farmers), plowmen and laborers, with a few car-

9 Ibid.
10 Grand Jury Presentments, Kershaw District, October Term, 1831; Lancaster District, Fall Term, 1849.

COMPARISON OF FREE BLACK AND WHITE AGRICULTURAL CONDITIONS
IN ABBEVILLE, BARNWELL AND RICHLAND DISTRICTS

	ABBEVILLE		BARNWELL		RICHLAND	
	White	Free Black	White	Free Black	White	Free Black
Population	12,699	357	12,289	311	6,764	501
Acres—improved land	212,628	558	197,676	1,296	89,426	569
Acres—unimproved land	425,031	336	957,393	2,547	235,695	182
Cash Value	4,740,923	2,750	2,746,605	9,046	2,006,777	1,736
Value, farming machinery	265,687	668	131,149	1,010	68,275	251
Horses	6,043	36	4,660	38	1,348	20
Asses and mules	2,875	4	1,868	2	1,643	19
Milch cows	8,282	36	10,410	83	3,051	66
Other cattle	16,242	54	23,908	208	8,459	181
Swine	66,548	211	68,303	495	19,163	310
Value, livestock	997,473	3,209	687,199	4,045	454,594	5,033
Bushels, wheat	99,101	181	10,866	288	6,538	
Bushels, Indian Corn	1,054,233	2,195	839,629	3,531	433,998	3,285
400 lb. bales ginned cotton	27,192	49	10,138	20	11,365	5

penters and blacksmiths.[11] Opportunity, however, was not
closed to the rural free black. In Marlboro District, for
instance, William Scott, a rafthand, had become a full-
fledged boatswain by the time he was thirty. He had a
large white clientele who looked after his interests and
helped establish his economic independence.[12]

Avenues for economic activity were much wider, of
course, in the city. Indeed, urban life held so many advantages that there was a constant stream of migration to
Charleston and other urban areas throughout the antebellum period. Economic activity in the city always maintained a high demand for labor. Slaves hiring their time
in Charleston provided a vast labor base, which in turn
gave an impetus to industry and trade. The free black was
able to exploit this cycle and compete successfully with
both the white mechanic and the slave. In fact, the institution of slavery helped him considerably, for white employers were accustomed to slave-labor and preferred to
hire the black rather than the white laborer, even in trades
that were markedly different from the plantation system.
The legislature recognized this tendency; thus while legislative action might tax the free black artisan and take his
profits from him, it never deprived him of his means of
livelihood. In 1858, the Committee on the Colored Population reported that "We are a slave-holding people habitual to slave labor. Yet we have towns and villages
where ordinary labor is to be performed . . . by either
white or negro hands. We are accustomed to black labor,
and it would create a revolution to drive it away."[13]

The free black actually occupied an intermediate position in the labor market. On the one hand, he had to

[11] Unpublished Agricultural Schedules of the Seventh Census.

[12] Marlboro County, S.C., Record of Deeds, H 1, 1813–19 (Microfilm),
South Carolina Archives Department.

[13] Report of the Committee on the Colored Population, Dec. 7, 1858,
in Reports of Committees of the South Carolina Legislature.

compete with slaves hiring their time, who were provided for by their masters and could therefore afford to work for lower wages. On the other hand, the free black was always paid less than the competing white mechanic and his labor was therefore in greater demand.[14] This situation gave rise to numerous protests from white artisans, who petitioned as early as 1783 against "Jobbing Negroe Tradesman, who undervalue Work by undertaking it for very little more than the Materials would cost."[15] The white mechanics were frequently driven to organize in order to meet the challenge, and their cause was sometimes taken up by local bodies of white citizens. In 1858, mechanics and workingmen of Charleston resolved "at a large and enthusiastic meeting of their body" to petition the legislature against competition by free blacks, but although the petition was signed by 161 workers, the effort availed them little.[16]

Another petition, signed by sixty-four citizens, many of whom were professionals, reveals a concern of a slightly different nature:

They [free black artisans] are rapidly drawing from the country the valuable class of industrious mechanics on whose intelegence and hardihood the safety of So. Carolina must mainly depend. What will be the condition of the State when your carpenters and painters and Blacksmiths, the occupants of all the departments of mechanical industry are free men of color, Yet such must be the consequence of the competition which the white mechanic encounters from the colored laborers. . . . Your petitioners cannot believe that you will per-

---

[14] Theodore D. Jervey, *Robert Y. Hayne and His Times*, p. 201.

[15] Petition of House Carpenters and Bricklayers of Charleston, Feb. 10, 1783, in Petitions Relating to Slavery.

[16] Petition of "The Society of Master Coopers of Charleston," 1793, in Petitions Relating to Slavery; Grand Jury Presentments, Charleston County, September Term, 1795, October Term, 1858; Petition of Charleston Mechanics and Workingmen, 1858, in Petitions Relating to Slavery.

mit a class so useless, pernicious and degrading to the character of the State, to supplant the intelligent industrious and rigorous freemen, who in the various mechanical departments, would so effectually increase her physical and moral strength.[17]

The petition is rather reminiscent of the neo-Jeffersonian appeal made in 1822 by "Achates"[18] for a society of frugal and industrious farmers and artisans, now threatened by the prototype of a rising black proletariat. The appeal may also have had some political overtones. In strongly Federalist Charleston, the new political challengers complained "that cheap negro labor was steadily undermining that class of Charleston's population which had ever been stridently Republican."[19]

These appeals were not unheeded. In Charleston, new city ordinances tended progressively to restrict the free black's economic activity. Thus blacks could not sell their produce without a license, and all sales were to be held only in the public market. No black could own a boat, save a fisherman who must then have a license for fishing. (This ordinance prevented free black pilots and seamen from plying their trades independently.) The city even imposed a ceiling on the free black's wages. For a full day's labor (i.e., from sunrise to sunset, allowing an hour each for breakfast and dinner), the black was to be paid a dollar; the rate for less than a day's labor was 12.5¢ an hour. If the free black demanded or received any higher wage he would be tried by the wardens of the city and on conviction pay five dollars or be confined in the workhouse until the fine was paid.[20] These restrictions were un-

---

[17] Petition of Certain Citizens of St. Helena's Parish, Beaufort District for the Removal of Free Negroes, n.d., in Petitions Relating to Slavery.

[18] Achates, *Reflections Occasioned by the Late Disturbances in Charleston, by Achates*, p. 12. The authorship of the pamphlet has been attributed to Thomas Pinckney.

[19] Jervey, *Hayne and His Times*, p. 130.

[20] *A Digest of the Ordinances of the City Council*, pp. 171–77.

doubtedly harsh; they tended, however, to be dead letters of the law, and the free blacks were able to pursue their trades unmolested for the most part. *The Directory and Stranger's Guide for the City of Charleston,* for instance, lists Primus Swain, a free black, among the "Pilots for the Bar and Harbor of Charleston" for the year 1819. His grade was "full branch" (i.e., independent, as distinct from apprentices, boat-keepers and twelve-foot-branch seamen), and he had served forty-two years, the longest period of service registered in the list.[21]

The Directory and Strangers Guide, which was published annually, provides some indication of the range of occupations followed by free blacks. The *Directory* for 1794, the earliest available, lists a number of free blacks in some very reputable occupations. Included were Francis Kinloch, planter; Thomas Ingliss and George Creighton, both hairdressers; Isaac Emmanuel, vendue master; Jehu Jones, manager of Jones' Long Room and a boarding-house, his wife Abby, a pastry cook, and their son Jehu Jones, Jr., a tailor; Thomas Bonneau, who ran a colored children's school on Beaufain Street; and Ann Akin, manager of a boarding school on Church Street.[22] Few of these trades were maintained by 1819. Jehu Jones' hotel continued to hold its own until 1823 when he left the state, but men like Jones and Primus Swain, the pilot, were remarkable exceptions. Their like was not seen in the period after 1830, due in part, of course, to the increasingly repressive environment in which the free black operated.

Most of Charleston's free blacks were cooks, seamstresses, mantuamakers, carpenters and barbers, all of them skilled

[21] *The Directory and Stranger's Guide for the City of Charleston, Also a Directory for Charleston Neck, Between Boundary Street and the Lines, For the Year 1819.*

[22] *The Directory and Stranger's Guide, for the City of Charleston, For*

artisans. Occupations of a different sort predominated among the free blacks of Charleston Neck, the newly developing area which was fast becoming a black ghetto. Here, a large number of blacks were unskilled laborers—carters, bricklayers and washers—and were less independent economically.[23] As the numerous petitions against them indicate, free black prostitutes plied a thriving trade among their white and colored clientele, but they were, of course, not listed in the *Directory*.

The *Directory*, in fact, is not an entirely satisfactory index to the economic activity of free blacks, since it was compiled by private individuals who did not have contact with the mass of the free black population. The city council, however, maintained what was called a "Free Negro Book," or list of blacks who paid poll tax. Although tax defaulters were very common, the lists are more complete than those compiled in the *Directory*. The Free Negro Book for 1823, for instance, lists 680 free blacks between the ages of 18 and 50, of whom 231 were employed in 35 different trades. The schedule below indicates the range and distribution of these trades.[24]

Carpenters	43	Coopers	5	Factors	1
Tailors	28	Coachmen	5	Sawyers	1
Laborers	28	Porters	4	Cigarmakers	1
Seamstresses	15	Servants	4	Cooks	1
Shoemakers	14	Carters	3	Umbrellamakers	1
Apprentices	12	Hairdressers	2	Tanners	1
Draymen	11	Mariners	2	Riggers	1
Waiters	10	Wheelwrights	2	Gardeners	1
Butchers	9	Chairmakers	2	Tinners	1
Fishermen	7	Schoolmasters	1	Turners	1
Barbers	6	Millwrights	1	Bricklayers	1
Cabinet-makers	5	Candlemakers	1		

23 *Charleston Directory*, 1819.
24 Free Negro Book, Comptroller General, 1823.

Not all the artisans listed were independent, but there were many among them who maintained a well-established family tradition and were in very prosperous material circumstances. The Holloways' Harness Shop and Carpenter's Establishment, for instance, had been founded in the late eighteenth century and employed a number of hired hands and apprentices. When Daniel Payne's parents left him destitute, he started out as an apprentice in the carpenter's shop of his brother-in-law, James Holloway. When he was finally able to fend for himself, he writes, "I raised money by making tables, benches, clotheshorses and 'corset-bones' which I sold on Saturday night in the public market."[25] Jonathan Baxter learned the shoemaker's trade from his father and was able to establish himself comfortably in Charleston.[26] But both Payne and Baxter had the advantage of training and support from their relatives. The average free black artisan had to create his market and fight to survive in the competing mass of free blacks, slaves and white artisans, and his place in the labor market was not always assured. Unlike the slave, however, his earnings were his own, and, in this at least, he enjoyed a clear advantage.

Of a very different order was the class of *rentiers* who rose to positions of wealth and affluence through speculation in land, banks and sometimes even slaves, as the following document indicates:

Received Charleston June 7th 1827 of Mr R[ichard] H[olloway] $42 for interest due on man Jack.

Sgd. Ann Mitchell[27]

---

[25] The Holloway Scrapbook; Daniel A. Payne, *Recollections of Seventy Years*, p. 18.
[26] George B. Tindall, *South Carolina Negroes*, p. 56.
[27] Holloway Scrapbook.

This is not to suggest, however, that members of this free black group were slave traders. The impulsions of a free market economy merely found new avenues for enterprise in the intimate domestic transactions of the family.[28] The same impulsion for profit led the free black to speculate in real estate, a lucrative enterprise in a developing area. Jehu Jones began his career as a tailor, possessed of a small house on Coming Street which had been deeded him by his mother, a woman of some means. In the early 1800s, he began to acquire land in Wraggsboro, a new township, and in Logan and Beaufain streets, where the value of land was steadily rising. In 1809 he bought a site on Broad Street, and in 1815 the house adjacent to it, which he mortgaged immediately. Thus began Jones' Lot, which expanded into Jones' Long Room and eventually became the famed Jones' Hotel.[29] The hotelier had a considerable asset in his wife, an excellent pastry cook, but not all free black pastry cooks made their way up to establishments on Broad Street. Jones also held shares in the Planters' and Mechanic's Bank in Charleston. On his death his estate was valued at over $40,000.[30]

The village of Hampstead, which had been chartered in 1816 in the northernmost part of the city, offered a rich source of investment for those who had the means. Well-established artisans like Richard Holloway, Thomas Bonneau, Joseph and Richard Dereef and Thomas Small were active in speculation in Charleston's frontier. Small's enterprise appears to have assumed large-scale proportions,

[28] Ann Mitchell and Richard Holloway were relatives. I have used this example to indicate how the profit motive sometimes dominated even family relationships.

[29] Register of Mesne Conveyance, B-8, pp. 202–3, X-7, pp. 262–64, M-8, pp. 399–403, L-7, p. 1, F-7, pp. 187–88, R-7, p. 196.

[30] Charleston Mercury, Sept. 27, 1822; F. C. Adams, Manuel Pereira, p. 89.

for he already possessed valuable sites in the city (one of which, Small's Court, still bears his name), and his activities as mortgagee were prolific. One particular transaction marks him as a man of considerable acumen. On February 28, 1845, Small bought a plot of land on Morris Street for $100; he sold it the next day for $500, making a profit of $400 overnight. Men of fewer means than Small could look to their mutual-aid societies for resources. Members of the Brown Fellowship Society were able to borrow money from its treasury at 20 percent interest to tide them over periods of financial stress or make improvements in their homes and businesses.[31]

This type of credit-union activity indicates that the free black was aware of the crucial importance of speculative enterprise in his struggle to get ahead. Speculation was the one avenue in which the black could compete on an equal level with the white. It was a fertile field of endeavor, and almost all free blacks possessing the means speculated in land, ignoring the state's incipient industrial enterprise, which entailed greater risks and more strenuous competition from white entrepreneurs, who had access to favors from the state. For the most part these propertied free blacks constituted a self-conscious economic interest in the state: as a *rentier* class they were not only quick to exploit opportunities for speculation but also quick to defend their interests against inroads made by the legislature and the tax collector.[32]

The degree of economic success among free blacks

[31] Register of Mesne Conveyance, F-10, pp. 65–70, K-9, pp. 359–60, B-12, pp. 250–52, 598–600, D-12, p. 242, B-10, pp. 122–23, Q-13, pp. 121–22, X-13, pp. 46, 73, H-13, p. 633, O-14, pp. 168–69, G-14, pp. 192–93, O-12, p. 535, L-12, pp. 339–40, H-13, pp. 575, 577; James B. Browning, "The Beginnings of Insurance Enterprise among Negroes," p. 426.

[32] Petition of free Negroes for Repeal of Capitation Tax Insofar as It Relates To Those Who Possess Property and Pay Tax Thereon, n.d., in Petitions Relating to Slavery.

varied, of course, with the different classes, but a common yardstick may be used to indicate the measure of success among the free black group in general. The usual indices to wealth in antebellum South Carolina were landed property and slaveholdings. In 1859, in Charleston alone, 353 out of 3,785 free blacks paid taxes on real estate valued at $778,000. The percentage of free black property holders (9 percent) compared favorably with the white population, of whom 17 percent paid taxes on real estate. Within this free black group, nine persons each paid taxes on over $10,000 worth of real estate.[33] The figures indicate that while a comparatively large number of free blacks owned real estate, a greater part of that property was concentrated in the hands of a few. The property-holding elite included men like Thomas Bonneau, who left a plantation and six houses at his death, and Richard Holloway, who, in the course of a very lucrative career as carpenter and real-estate speculator, acquired twenty-two houses, many of which, located in the best localities, were rented out to white citizens. Also comparable was the wealth of Jane Wightman, whose four-acre farm in Charleston was valued at $3,000 and her house and lot on Chalmers Street at $7,000.[34] A fair amount of the total wealth was distributed also among the smaller artisans in the city. For instance, the real estate of Florin Long, a bootmaker, was valued at $5,000, while William Seymour, a tavernkeeper, William Stevens, a porter, and Felicity White, a shopkeeper, owned real estate valued at $3,000,

[33] John Hope Franklin, *From Slavery to Freedom,* p. 221; E. Horace Fitchett, "The Free Negro in Charleston South Carolina," p. 86.

[34] Will of Thomas Bonneau, Record of Wills (Charleston County), Vol. 39, Book C, 1826–34, pp. 905–7; Will of Richard Holloway, ibid., Vol. 43, Book B, 1839–45, pp. 891–95; Will of Jane Wightman, ibid., Vol. 46, Book A, 1851–56, pp. 258–60; Seventh Census, Charleston District, South Carolina Archives; Unpublished Agricultural Schedules of the Seventh Census (Charleston District).

$2,000 and $1,500 respectively. The favorable locations of these properties, more than their extensiveness, account for their high values.[35] The great majority of free blacks, of course, owned no land at all.

A similar distribution is evident in the schedule of slaveholders in the city. Of 360 free colored slaveholders in 1860, 130 were taxed on 390 slaves.[36] A few free blacks owed their fortunes to heavy investments in slaves. When Abraham Jackson, a freed slave, made his will in 1785, he admitted leaving a plantation heavily encumbered by debt. But the planter anticipated that the labor of his slaves would yield enough income to settle his debts and make annual payments "unto my several relations vix. My wife Daphne, my Nephews Abraham and Jack and my Nieces Elsey, Dolly and Sally."[37] In somewhat similar circumstances, Rebecca Jackson directed her executors to sell her slaves at public auction, "discharging from the proceeds arising from such Sale all my just debts and funeral charges and also the Several Specific Legacies above mentioned [eight legacies amounting to $440]." The good lady even anticipated that when all was settled there would be a surplus, which she directed to be distributed equally among her four children.[38]

In some very outstanding cases, the wealth of free blacks was directed beyond the individual to the family or the coterie of upper-class free blacks who sustained one another through associations and insurance organizations. The estate of Maria Creighton was bequeathed in trust to

[35] Seventh Census, Parish of St. Philip's and St. Michael's, Ward I, Charleston District, ibid.

[36] Carter G. Woodson, *Free Negro Heads of Families,* p. xxxiv.

[37] Will of Abraham Jackson, Record of Wills, Vol. 22, Book A, 1786–93 (Charleston County), pp. 67–68.

[38] Will of Rebecca Jackson, ibid., Vol. 42, Book B, 1839–45 (Charleston County), pp. 222–24.

the Baptist church of Charleston with the specific injunction that it be used to support poor blacks in the city.
George Creighton, another free black, financed the migration of his slaves when he left for Liberia in 1821.[39] Some
enterprising free blacks contributed to the wealth and
prestige of the entire state. During the exigencies of the
American Revolution, Joe Farquarson, a free black, lent
£1,510 sterling to the state of South Carolina, supplement-
ing the effort made by free blacks enlisted in the Revolutionary armies.[40]

The fame of South Carolina's free blacks sometimes
went well beyond the state. Travelers in South Carolina
were well acquainted with the hotel of Jehu Jones, of
whom it was said:

His house was unquestionably the best in the city and had a
widespread reputation. Few persons of note ever visited
Charleston without putting up at Jones', where they found not
only the comforts of a private house, but a table spread with
every luxury that the country afforded. The Governor always
put up at Jones', and when you were travelling abroad, strangers would speak of the sumptuous fare at Jones' in Charleston
and the elegance and correctness of his house.

Jones also owned a hotel on Sullivan's Island, a fashionable
resort for Charleston's crème de la crème. He was well-
respected in Charleston and every inch a gentleman, even
to the point of suffering from gout! Thomas Hamilton,
the fastidious English traveler, appears to have been so
impressed by the man's hospitality that he strongly recommended that "Every Englishman who visits Charleston,

---

[39] Will of Maria Creighton, ibid., Vol. 39, Book C, 1826–34 (Charleston
County), pp. 1,176–79; Woodson, *Free Negro Heads of Families*, p. xxxv.
[40] Receipt by Commissioners of the Public Treasury, from a free Negro
named Joe, Mar. 27, 1779, in Miscellaneous Records.

will, if he be wise, direct his baggage to be conveyed to Jones' hotel."[41]

Jones had to contend with strong competition from another of Charleston's free blacks, Eliza Lee, who owned the "Mansion House" on the same street. Mrs. Lee bequeathed the state something more tangible than a reputation for good cooking. According to tradition, her two sons went North to seek their fortunes, and, when hardship threatened, resorted to the art their mother had taught them. News of their methods for pickling and preserving soon reached the ears of an enterprising man named Heinz, who bought their recipes and rights. South Carolina's contribution to the "57 Varieties" distributed today by J. H. Heinz & Company thus goes back over a hundred years to a very enterprising free black woman who was, even then, an asset to the state.[42]

The free black population in South Carolina was not a sizable one. Even when its numbers were largest, it never exceeded 2 percent of the total population. By comparison with its numbers, however, the economic contribution made by the free black group was more than considerable. The free blacks were not, as a South Carolina judge once described them, "drones and lazaroni—consumers, without being producers."[43] Records for the poorhouse show that the proportion of free blacks lodged there was always

---

[41] Adams, *Manuel Pereira*, p. 89; Karl Bernard, Duke of Saxe-Weimar Eisenach, *Travels Through North America during the Years 1825 and 1826*, II, pp. 4–5; Mrs. St. Julien Ravenal, *Charleston, the Place and the People*, p. 459; Thomas Hamilton, *Men and Manners in America*, pp. 347–48; *Charleston Mercury*, May 14, 1823.

[42] A room taken out of the "Mansion House" is installed in the Henry Francis Du Pont Winterthur Museum, near Wilmington, Delaware, where it is still used as a dining room for entertaining guests. Miss Helen McCormack, Director, Gibbes Art Gallery, Charleston, to the author, Feb. 1, 1966.

[43] Helen T. Catterall, ed., *Judicial Cases Concerning American Slavery and the Negro*, II, pp. 441–42.

small in comparison with the white and slave populations. Even the large group of free black women were rarely dependents, for the majority of them were engaged in a variety of skilled trades.[44] Insofar as free blacks supported themselves, they proved less of an economic burden to the state than its white citizenry. Beyond that, the free blacks supported the state through taxation and sustained its economic life by their activities in the fields of speculation and entrepreneurship. It was in these fields, unencumbered by legal and social disabilities, that they were able to fulfill themselves, and it was in this area that they contributed most markedly to the stability of the state.

[44] Records of the Poor House; Free Negro Book, 1823; *Charleston Directory*, 1823. Free black women often registered in the Free Negro Book as "dependents" in order to avoid the city tax on black tradesmen. A comparison with the *Directory* for the same years reveals that a majority of them were seamstresses, cooks or mantua makers.

CHAPTER VI

Black Religion

RELIGION WAS THE HUB IN THE ANTEBELLUM BLACK'S life. The social life of the white population was distributed over a range of activities, from the debutante ball to the unrestrained conviviality of the local tavern. Even the rural "redneck," whose emotional orgies at the weekly revivalist meeting made up for a cheerless day-to-day existence, could find some comfort in the life which centered around his family, his crops, a visit to the country store and, perhaps, an occasional barbecue. The slave had none of these institutions and pastimes. With the exception of a few favored house servants, the slave's existence was geared toward the profits of the plantation system; and the techniques of labor control did not quite aspire to self-fulfillment. Religion filled the void. In the weekly services and class meetings the slaves entered a different world, where they met and talked freely, sang, danced, chanted, "witnessed" and found social consolation in the fostering of one another's souls.

The free black was closely associated with the slave in his religious activity, for the delineation of segregated congregations, located in the galleries of white churches, made no distinction between the slave and the free colored man. But it was more than physical proximity which drew the free black into the religious life of the slave population. The same inadequacy in his social life as in the slave's led him to rely on the church for the fulfillment of his social needs. In rural areas, isolated free blacks sought the company of slaves, and both groups, like the white yeoman farmer, found the church to be the only real channel for social intercourse. The city provided more opportunity, but even here all gatherings, whether in the marketplace, the tavern or the home, were strictly under the surveillance of the city patrol. It was only at the church meeting that the blacks could legitimately come together, subject to the legal requirement that at least one white person should be present at the gathering.[1] Even among the free black upper class, whose social life was more sophisticated, family prayers, burial societies and benevolent church organizations were developed with a view to stabilizing social institutions. The church thus provided an avenue for self-expression and the growth of a sense of community within the free black group.

Religious activity among the black population began very early. The Church of England's Society for the Propagation of the Gospel in Foreign Parts sent its missionaries to South Carolina in 1702. The weather they encountered was warmer than the reception they received. The South Carolina planter not only resented the threatened disruption of his slave's tranquillity, but there was also evidently some confusion in his mind as to whether baptism made the slave a freeman. The spiritually sophisticated missionaries soon cleared the hurdle, however, with some assist-

[1] *A Digest of the Ordinances of the City Council of Charleston For the years 1783 to October, 1844*, pp. 176–77.

ance from the Lords Proprietors of the province. In 1712, an act passed by the assembly declared: "Since charity and the christian religion, which we profess, oblige us to wish well to the souls of all men, and that religion may not be made a pretence to alter any man's property and right, and that no person may neglect to baptize their negroes or slaves or suffer them to be baptized, for fear that thereby they should be manumitted . . . such slave or slaves [who] shall receive and profess the christian religion . . . shall not thereby be manumitted or set free."[2] The act failed to reassure the planters, however, and opposition was manifested particularly against the efforts of the missionaries to educate the slave. The proselytizers eventually compromised, confining their methods of teaching to sermons, conversations and oral instruction.[3]

Having neither state nor planter to interpose in their personal lives, the earliest free blacks must have provided a fruitful field for missionary endeavor. Their receptivity to conversion may have brightened an otherwise discouraging task. The Reverend William Guy, who served in St. Andrew's Parish for twenty-two years beginning in 1719, reported that free blacks predominated in his colored flock. In 1746 the Reverend William Orr reported to the S.P.G. that he had been preparing adult blacks for baptism, "a work of no small labor and difficulty," he complained, "considering the aversion which many of their owners have to any such thing." In 1748 he had some progress to report: "Since my Last I have baptized two free nigroe Women after proper Instruction, both of them

[2] Frank J. Klingberg, *An Appraisal of the Negro in Colonial South Carolina*, pp. 4, 13–14; David J. McCord and Thomas Cooper, eds., *The Statutes At Large of South Carolina*, VII, pp. 364–65, hereafter referred to as *Statutes At Large*.

[3] Klingberg, *Negro in Colonial South Carolina*, p. 5.

very sensible and sober; and each of them answered to the full Satisfaction, when examined concerning their Belief, and expressed their sincere Desire to be admitted into the Christian Church by the Holy Sacrament of Baptised. . . ."[4]

Free blacks were the beneficiaries of the Charleston Negro School, established in 1743 by the Reverend Alexander Garden. Originally intending that the school should be run independently by slaves, Garden insisted that its maintenance "must be by *Negro* Schoolmasters, Homeborn, and equally Property as other slaves." Two boys were bought and trained as teachers to begin with, and the school flourished for a while, producing forty-two scholars between 1745 and 1747. The Anglican priest wrote to the S.P.G. repeatedly for books, warning it against the fundamentalist proclivities of his charges. The society responded in the hope that the success of the school would eventually lead to a state-supported school for blacks. Misfortune befell the effort, however. Andrew, the "slower Genius" of the two teachers, proved a failure and was resold in 1750. Soon after, the society discontinued its funds to the school, and when Harry, the second teacher, died in 1764, the effort collapsed. That the free blacks benefited from the project was due largely to a continuing opposition from the planters which kept the number of slave recruits low. The education students received was strictly religious and Anglican; graduating scholars were not only capable of reading the Bible but had also been well instructed in the church catechism.[5]

After the Revolution, the Anglican missionary effort among the blacks was supplanted by that of the Baptist, Presbyterian and Methodist churches, although the new

[4] Ibid., pp. 62, 81.
[5] Ibid., pp. 102–19.

Episcopal church continued to be active among the blacks in Charleston.[6] Of all the denominations, by far the most successful was the Methodist. It has been said that such was the response of South Carolina's slaves to Methodism that Episcopalian planters often employed Methodist ministers on their plantations.[7] Methodist roots in South Carolina went back to 1736 when John and Charles Wesley visited Charleston and John Wesley preached in St. Philip's Church at the invitation of Reverend Garden. Wesley was impressed by the presence of blacks in the church and stressed the need for missionary work among the black population. His work was revived by George Whitefield, who visited Charleston in 1738 and again in 1769. But it was not until 1785 that the first Methodist church was established in South Carolina. Members met, somewhat inappropriately, in a deserted Baptist meeting-house. The Methodists enjoyed an immense popularity with South Carolina blacks from the very beginning. In 1787 an increase of 53 was reported in the colored congregation, while the whites registered no increase. In 1791, there were 119 blacks and 66 whites; in 1793, 280 blacks and 65 whites; and by 1815, 3,793 blacks and 282 whites.[8]

The Methodist appeal was complex and varied. One of the church's greatest attractions, perhaps, was its reputation in regard to slavery. John Wesley had attacked the institution in a pamphlet published in 1774, entitled *Thoughts on Slavery*, in which he portrayed the African as the perfect embodiment of Natural Man, and the outcome of his publication had been the decision of the American Methodist Conference in 1790 that slaveholding was

[6] Luther P. Jackson, "The Religious Instruction of Negroes, 1830 to 1860, with Special Reference to South Carolina."

[7] Interview with Mr. Samuel Stoney, Charleston, July 17, 1965.

[8] F. A. Mood, *Methodism in Charleston*, pp. 10–20, 23–24, 40, 48, 71, 128.

contrary to the laws of God and man.[9] But the average black in South Carolina was not likely to comprehend the decisions of the national conference, still less to hear of them. At any rate, he would have found this posture hard to reconcile with the segregated congregations that the Methodists continued to maintain in the South, in keeping with the practice of other denominations. What was of perhaps more fundamental appeal to the black was the inherently chiliastic outlook of Methodist teaching, concerned as it was with preparing the souls of men for the life hereafter. It injected meaning and purpose into an otherwise incomprehensible state of bondage. It transferred the slave's attention from the sweat and tears, the public auction and the sundered family to that eternal reward and reunion in heaven. It was as Karl Mannheim has so aptly expressed it, "the hope of the dispirited and the defeated."[10]

Methodist meetings, as did most fundamentalist services, carried strong undercurrents of emotionalism which, often enough, culminated in violent outbursts of hysteria. Travelers in the South were invariably moved to comment on the pitch of excitement which seemed to prevail in particular at black prayer meetings. One visitor, bemused at the shrieking, stamping, clapping and dancing to which the black worshippers surrendered themselves, thought he detected a carry-over of an inherently heathen experience. But the mass hysteria was not unprovoked, as the observer admitted. Methodist ministers were well acquainted with the superstitious mentality of the common people among

---

9 Maldwyn Edwards, *After Wesley*, pp. 64–65.

10 Mannheim observes that these promises of a better land, removed in time and place, are like checks that cannot be cashed: their only function is to provide escape from the situation of struggle to which the individual actually belongs. Karl Mannheim, *Ideology and Utopia: An Introduction to the Sociology of Knowledge*, p. 218.

whom they had the most numerous recruits. Early Methodism in England, for instance, had found its greatest support among colliers, tin miners, cotton weavers and factory workers—simple men who were beginning to experience the dislocations of a growing industrial system. The Methodist meetings provided an outlet for the tensions developing among these groups. Worshippers were encouraged to give utterance to their thoughts, their desires and experiences, to "speak freely," to confess their faults, repent and bear witness, all this to the accompaniment of sensuous projections by the preacher of hellfire and eternal damnation.[11] The slave found the outlet welcome. The Methodist church redirected his emotions from his repressive daily life and social situation into the limitless avenue of religious experience. Worship thus became an event where preacher, steward, class leader and class member alike gave themselves up to the workings of the Spirit.

Methodism's appeal, however, included more positive aspects. The Methodist church was less concerned with teaching than with providing its members with a share of responsibility. In the administrative hierarchy, blacks served as lay preachers, stewards and class leaders, and as they gained in administrative experience, they grew in stature. Frederick Law Olmsted noted during his travels in South Carolina that "The office among the negroes, as among all other people, confers a certain importance and power. A part of the reverence attaching to the duties is given to the person; vanity and self-confidence are culti-

---

[11] Frederick Law Olmsted, *The Cotton Kingdom: A Traveller's Observations on Cotton and Slavery in the American Slave States,* I, pp. 259, 271; Robert F. Wearmouth, *Methodism and the Common People of the Eighteenth Century* (London, 1945), pp. 177, 185–86; Robert F. Wearmouth, *Methodism and the Working Class Movements of England,* pp. 13–21.

vated, and a higher ambition aroused than can usually
enter the mind of a slave."[12]

The free blacks had many opportunities for leadership
in the Methodist church, for they were unhampered by the
restrictions of slave discipline. The Methodist-Episcopal
Church, an offshoot of—and more Methodist than—the
Episcopal, enjoyed remarkable success through the me-
dium of free black lay preachers. Bishop William Capers
recognized the importance of their role when he wrote,
"We had belonging to the Church in Charleston, as if
raised up for the exigencies of the time [1811], some ex-
traordinary [free] colored men. I have mentioned Castle
Selby; there were also Amos Baxter, Tom Smith, Peter
Simpson, Smart Simpson, Harry Bull, Richard Holloway,
Alek [sic] Harlston and others, men of intelligence and
piety, who read the Scriptures and understood them, and
were zealous for religion among the Negroes." He added,
"They were the only persons who for Christ's sake were
zealous enough to undertake such a service, and who at
the same time could get access to the people that the
service might be rendered."[13]

The impact of such participation on the free black cannot be overstressed. Accustomed to a position of subordination, and ruled rather than ruling, the free black found
in the church his first opportunity to fulfill his capacity for
leadership. Methodism revolutionized his status. Basically
social in its outlook, it brought the free black class leader
into close contact with the mass of slaves and free blacks,
among whom he came to be their acknowledged leader.
Among the vast numbers arrested for complicity in the
Vesey "uprising" were many who were acknowledged by

[12] Olmsted, *The Cotton Kingdom*, I, p. 260.
[13] William M. Wightman, *The Life of William Capers*, p. 138; The
Holloway Scrapbook; Daniel A. Payne, *Recollections of Seventy Years*,
p. 17; William J. Simmons, *Men of Mark*, p. 811.

witnesses as leaders in the black community. With few exceptions, they were all class leaders.[14]

The Methodists met with a good deal of opposition, of course, much on the scale that they had encountered in England and much of it instigated by rival churches, in particular the Episcopal, always suspicious of rampant fundamentalism, and the Baptist, whose own fundamentalism seemed less attractive to the black.[15] In South Carolina, suspicions regarding the egalitarianism of the church were heightened by the issue of slavery. As early as 1789 one of the local Methodist ministers committed an unpardonable indiscretion in openly attacking the peculiar institution. The response, which was immediate, was only the opening shot in the battery against the church. "Methodists were watched, ridiculed and openly assailed," writes F. A. Mood. "Their churches were styled 'negro churches' and their preachers 'the negro preachers.'" Doors were barred to members of Methodist congregations on the grounds that "those who have turned the world upside down are come hither also." And South Carolinians' fears were hardly allayed when one of Charleston's well-known citizens on conversion plunged down East Bay yelling "Hallelujah" at the top of his lungs. It was altogether a tumultuous experience. Bishop Francis Asbury remarked with asperity that between the "awakenings" of the congregation inside the church and the riots outside it, "we had noise enough."[16]

The issue of slavery weighed heavily against the Methodist church, which soon began to lose its white members. In 1791 a quarrel which broke out between the bishop

[14] Document B, Documents Relating to the Vesey Uprising.

[15] Mood, *Methodism in Charleston*, p. 184; Petition of Sundry Baptist Churches, 1801, in Petitions Relating to Slavery.

[16] Wearmouth, *Methodism and the Common People*, pp. 140–41; Mood, *Methodism in Charleston*, pp. 43, 64, 28, 45.

and a minister led to the minister's withdrawal with half of the white congregation.[17] Thus isolated, the Methodists became the target of an anti-abolitionist campaign. Wild reports of abolitionists among the Methodist preachers led to even wilder riots in the course of which a Methodist minister was drowned under a spout.[18]

When the state finally stepped in to restore order, it was to remove what it thought was the root of disorder: the religious instruction of blacks. Acts passed in 1800 and 1803 declared their religious meetings held between sunset and sunrise to be illegal, while any meeting in the daytime was to consist of a majority of white people.[19] Those affected most by the acts were the Methodist congregations who had maintained separate class meetings conducted by blacks. The acts' immediate result was to break up these groups, but the laws were laxly enforced and within a few years class meetings and prayer groups resumed their work. They suffered, however, from frequent invasions by the patrol and could find little protection, even in cases of unwarranted interference, for it was commonly believed by judge and jury alike that "the Patrol Law . . . ought to be considered as one of the safeguards of the people of South Carolina, for the protection of their dwellings . . . and as security against insurrection; a danger of such a nature, that it never can or ought to be lost sight of in the southern states."[20] If it offered any consolation to the evangelists, however, the Methodists continued to violate the laws with the same impunity with which the patrol violated their rights. In 1834, appealing for a more realistic law, the evangelists acknowledged that "the people of

[17] Mood, *Methodism in Charleston,* pp. 54–61, 71.
[18] Ibid., pp. 87–91.
[19] *Statutes At Large,* VII, pp. 442–43, 448–49.
[20] Helen T. Catteral, ed., *Judicial Cases Concerning American Slavery and the Negro,* II, p. 316.

color have for thirty years been indulged with the privilege of religious instruction and worship after sunset and with less than a majority of white persons present. . . ."[21]

Black religious groups engaged in a variety of activities. They met weekly, both at prayer meetings and at smaller class meetings which were usually held in the homes of slaves or free blacks. According to the testimony in the Vesey trials, these meetings were more social than religious. The blacks discussed topical issues like the Missouri Controversy, prospects in Liberia and the newest scandals among the white aristocracy. The excitement their conversations provided did not keep them from the more mundane tasks of preaching the gospel and taking up collections for the poor, for which they were solely responsible. Black worshippers were also allowed to partake of the "love-feast," on a strictly segregated basis. Segregated though they were, the blacks in the Methodist church had more opportunity for participation in the affairs of the church than had been offered them by any other denomination. The "call" and the catechism held little luster beside the prospect of power and responsibility.[22]

This growing independence was consummated in the establishment of an African Methodist Episcopal church in Charleston in 1817. The A.M.E. Church, as it is commonly called, originated in 1787 in Philadelphia, when the colored members of St. George's Methodist Episcopal Church, suffering discrimination from the white members, withdrew. In 1793 the congregation set up an African Meeting under the leadership of Richard Allen, a charter

[21] A Bill for the more punctual performance of the patrol duty, 1819, Reports of Committees of the South Carolina Legislature; Petition from ministers in the parishes of St. Philip and St. Michael, ibid.; John Belton O'Neall, ed., *The Negro Law of South Carolina*, p. 13.

[22] Document B, Documents Relating to the Vesey Uprising; Mood, *Methodism in Charleston*, p. 75; Holloway Scrapbook.

member of the Free African Society, a welfare organization. Similar occurrences in Baltimore prompted the dissenters to form an Ecclesiastical Compact in 1816, when, with other dissident groups from Delaware, Pennsylvania and New Jersey, the A.M.E. Church was established.[23]

The Charleston branch of the church sprang out of a similar schism. In 1815, revisions in the Methodist regulations impinged upon the independence enjoyed so far by the colored congregations. The separate colored Quarterly Conferences were abolished, their collections thenceforth to be managed by white stewards, and church trials were thereafter to be conducted by the Methodist minister. The outcome was the withdrawal of 4,367 members led by Morris Brown, a free black lay preacher—over four-fifths of the entire black congregation. The effect was devastating. Reverend Mood recalled that "The galleries, hitherto crowded, were almost completely deserted, and it was a vacancy that could be felt."[24]

The protestants met temporarily in a hearse-house erected on a burial ground in Pitt Street. In 1817 they petitioned the legislature for permission to worship in a church they had built in Hampstead. Careful to assure the authorities of their good faith, the free black organizers of the church undertook to maintain certain conditions: "that the door of the church remain open always, and that all white ministers of the Gospel of every denomination shall be respectfully invited to officiate in the said Church, whenever disposed so to do, and that separate seats shall be provided for such citizens as may honor the congregation with their presence, either for religious instruction or to inspect their morals and deportment. That no minister

[23] [Daniel A. Payne?], *The History of the African Methodist Episcopal Church*, pp. 3–4; James B. Browning, "The Beginnings of Insurance Enterprise among Negroes," p. 418.
[24] Mood, *Methodism in Charleston*, pp. 130–32.

of color who does not reside in this State shall officiate for the said congregation, nor shall any slave be admitted a member thereof without the approbation of his or her owner. . . . That every exertion will be used . . . to preserve the utmost order and decorum."[25]

Despite such assurances, the Charleston delegation in the House recommended rejection of the petition on the grounds that "the petitioners would be better instructed by well educated and pious Divines in the Churches in that city than by ignorant and fanatical preachers of their own color. . . ."[26] But the group continued to meet as a legally constituted church and soon built up a sizable congregation. Church members were active in the A.M.E. organization in Philadelphia and a number of them were elected deacons and elders at the annual conferences, among whom were Morris Brown, Amos Cruikshanks, Henry Drayton, Smart Simpson and Aleck Harleston. Their acknowledged leader was Morris Brown, a wealthy man deeply committed to the cause of the black. He was not an eloquent preacher, and, as Daniel Payne recalled, "spoke very broken English." But his piety was genuine and his practical, almost rustic appeal to the blacks invoked more support than the terrifying predictions of hell and damnation had yet yielded.[27]

For a time the Charleston A.M.E. congregation, second only to that of Philadelphia in numbers, throve as slave

[25] Petition of certain free persons of color attached to the African Methodist Episcopal Church in Charleston called Zion, 1817, in Petitions Relating to Slavery; Petition of free people of color for authority to purchase two lots of land in Wraggsborough for a burial ground, 1817, ibid.; Register of Mesne Conveyance, A-9, pp. 236–39; Will of Christopher Williman, Record of Wills, Vol. 32, Book E (Charleston County), pp. 744–49.
[26] Report of the Charleston delegation to whom was referred the Petition of free persons of color of Mt. Zion Church, Dec. 2, 1817, in Reports of Committees of the South Carolina Legislature.
[27] [Payne?], History of the A.M.E. Church, pp. 21–27, 34, 262–65.

and free black, rich and poor, flocked to the first all-black association in the state. But the inevitable reaction was soon in coming. Opposition to the maintenance of the church is actually less surprising than the fact that its establishment was allowed at all. As Payne pointed out

The tendency of all . . . was to prove that the colored man was incapable of self-government and self-support. . . . But is not the existence of the A.M.E. Church a flat contradiction and triumphant refutation of this slander . . . ? Compelled to govern others, its ministry has been constrained to read and investigate church history for models of government; and to discriminate between laws which were just, and those which were unjust; to expunge from the statutes of the Church those which were unequal in their bearing and to substitute those of a more equable character. . . .[28]

In December 1817, soon after the church had begun to operate, a group of 469 blacks were arrested on charges of disorderly conduct, "they having bought a lot, erected a building and engaged therein in a species of worship which the neighborhood found a nuisance." In June 1818, 143 more were arrested; eight ministers were each sentenced to receive ten lashes or pay a fine of five dollars; and Morris Brown and four other prominent ministers were given the alternative of leaving the state or suffering one month's imprisonment.[29] Brown chose imprisonment, in spite of the authorities' obvious desire to be rid of him. But his troubles were not over.

In 1820 the sparks of the Missouri controversy ignited South Carolina. The subject of the clause in Missouri's proposed state constitution banning free blacks or mulat-

[28] Ibid., pp. 33, 10–11.
[29] City Gazette (Charleston), Dec. 4, 1817; Charleston Courier, June 9, 1818.

toes from entering the state was discussed, argued and judged by the learned and the unlearned, from the governor and legislature down to the commonest free black or slave. The legislature went so far as to endorse officially the constitution of Missouri, but it is the governor's message which best reflects the fears of the slaveholding population. The threat to the security of the state, he said, was threefold—federal interference, abolitionism and the growing number of free blacks. The latter two seemed to be embodied in the new African Methodist Episcopal church in Charleston, and it was soon singled out for attack. In 1820 a group of citizens petitioned the legislature against "existing evils among free negroes": a spacious new building recently erected for the exclusive worship of blacks, financed by abolition societies in the Northern and Eastern states; the permitting of free blacks to travel to the Eastern states for "ordination and other religious pretences"; the recruitment by the church of missionary schoolmasters from Philadelphia, "amply furnished with pecuniary means by abolition societies of that State, for the avowed purpose of educating our Negroes."[30]

The state responded with a stringent law against abolitionists and immigrant free blacks, but the charge of abolitionism could not be proved against the A.M.E. church. Then, as if by the designs of providence, the Denmark Vesey uprising presented the opportunity for a coup de grace. It transpired, in the course of the Vesey trials, that a large number of those implicated in the conspiracy were class leaders in the A.M.E. church. The court concluded

[30] Resolution of the House of Representatives, Dec. 9, 1820, in Reports of Committees of the South Carolina Legislature; Resolution of the Senate of South Carolina, Dec. 8, 1820, ibid.; Message No. 1 of Gov. John Geddes, Nov. 27, 1820, in Messages of the Governors of South Carolina to the Legislature; Petition of sundry citizens of Charleston to the House of Representatives, 1820, in Petitions Relating to Slavery.

that the plot originated in the church; the white churches enthusiastically endorsed the view; and the newspapers gave it publicity. On August 6, 1822, by a somewhat garbled interpretation of the Act of 1820, Morris Brown and Henry Drayton were found guilty of leaving the state and reentering it illegally and were ordered to leave South Carolina within fifteen days. Soon after, the church was dismantled on the orders of the city council.[31]

The rival churches did not pass over the discomfiture of the Methodists. The Reverend Richard Furman of the Baptist church, for reasons perhaps best known to himself, suggested a Day of Thanksgiving and Humiliation. The Reverend Frederick Dalcho noted with some satisfaction that none of the blacks involved in the conspiracy had belonged to the Episcopal church, which he attributed to the fact that in "the sober, rational, sublime and evangelical worship of the Protestant Episcopal Church, there is nothing to inflame the passions of the ignorant enthusiast, nothing left to the crude undigested ideas of illiterate black class-leaders." The Methodists evidently came to accept the conviction that teaching ought not to be left to class leaders. In 1845 the General Conference decided against allowing blacks to preach to fellow blacks.[32]

[31] Lionel H. Kennedy and Thomas Parker, *An Official Report of the Trials of Sundry Negroes, charged With an Attempt to raise an Insurrection in the State of South Carolina*, p. 23; James Hamilton, Jr., ed., *An Account of the Late Intended Insurrection Among A Portion of the Blacks of this City*, p. 30; *A South Carolinian* [Frederick Dalcho?], *Practical Considerations Founded on the Scriptures Relative to the Slave Population of South Carolina*, pp. 32–36; Richard Furman, *Exposition of the Views of the Baptists Relative to the Colored Population of the United States in a Communication to the Governor of South Carolina*, p. 17; *City Gazette* (Charleston), Aug. 10, 1822; Mood, *Methodism in Charleston*, p. 133.

[32] Furman, *Exposition*, p. 1; [Dalcho?], *Pratical Considerations Founded on the Scriptures*, p. 30; Howell Meadows Henry, *Police Control of the Slave in South Carolina*, pp. 140–41; *Proceedings of the Meeting in Charleston, South Carolina, May 13–15, 1845, on the Religious Instruction of the Negroes together with the Report of the Committee and the Address to the Public.*

Religious instruction of blacks continued, however, in the separate congregations of the regular churches. Even the Reverend Richard Furman's willingness to ascribe the "plot" to the African church stemmed, in part, from the need to emphasize the regular church as the proper avenue for religious functions, with the "proper" division of black and white. Evangelical zeal was tempered now with caution. The churches relied on verbal instruction through sermons, hymns and catechisms.[33] But well-known free black lay preachers like Richard Holloway continued to preach among the blacks, and their activity was not seriously challenged save when upheavals in neighboring states, like the rebellion of Nat Turner in Virginia, threw South Carolinians into alarm.[34]

As the errant blacks returned to the fold, the problem of accommodation became acute. The Methodists compromised temporarily by seating free blacks with the whites on the main floor, while the slaves occupied the galleries. But protests from white members made a permanent solution imperative. In 1844 the Methodist church set up a separate meeting house for the blacks, allotted them a portion of church property and debts and provided a separate preacher for them. The Presbyterians followed suit shortly after, although the decision provoked a public controversy and threatened a schism within the church. The matter was settled, however, when the Reverend James Henley Thornwell persuaded the white congregation that "Our own security is best consulted . . . by giv-

[33] Paul Trapier, *The Religious Instruction of the Black Population. The Gospel to be Given to Our Servants;* Charles Colcock Jones, *Suggestions on the Religious Instruction of the Negroes in the Southern States;* William Capers, *A Short Catechism For the Use of Colored Members on Trial in the Methodist Episcopal Church in South Carolina; A Catechism To be Used by Teachers in the Religious Instruction of Persons of Color in the Episcopal Church of South Carolina* [n.p.?, n.d.?].

[34] Holloway Scrapbook; Grand Jury Presentments, Richland District, October Term, 1831, Kershaw District, October Term, 1831.

ing it a wise direction and turning it into safe and salutary channels. Separate congregations . . . they *will* have. If our laws and the public sentiment of the community tolerate them, they will be open, public, responsible. If our laws prohibit them, they will be secret, fanatical, dangerous." Eventually a church was built for the blacks on Anson Street and expanded, later, on Boundary Street. The roles were reversed now, with the blacks occupying the main floor and the whites provided with galleries! Soon after, the Episcopal church established a congregation for the blacks under the direction of the Reverend Paul Trapier.[35]

These black congregations were by no means independent. They were still under the discipline of the white churches and their preachers were white. But they provided the antebellum black with valuable experience. When church organizations disintegrated under the impact of the Civil War, the blacks dissolved their ties with the white churches and set up their own organizations, on the foundations of former separate congregations. Thus originated the Camden Baptist Church, the A.M.E. church reestablished by Daniel Payne, and the Plymouth Congregational Church. Only St. Mark's Episcopal Church was established exclusively by free blacks, and it continued to maintain its connection with the white parent organization. Its founding members included the Dereefs, Benjamin Kinloch, and William McKinley, prominent figures in Charleston's free black elite.[36]

[35] Mood, *Methodism in Charleston*, pp. 144–49; John B. Adger, *My Life and Times, 1810–1899*, pp. 169, 170, 172–75.

[36] George B. Tindall, *South Carolina Negroes*, pp. 187–90; Payne, *Recollections; Church Annual of the Plymouth Congregational Church;* interview with the Rev. John T. Enwright, Charleston, July 14, 1965; *Souvenir Program of the One-Hundredth Anniversary of the Founding of the A.M.E. Church in the South held at Emmanuel A.M.E. Church*, pp. 3–6; *Some Historical Facts about St. Mark's Episcopal Church*, pp. 1–2.

The Reverend Morris Brown died in exile in Philadelphia and did not live to see his creation fulfilled. Some of Charleston's blacks now worship in a church on Morris Street commonly called "Morris Brown A.M.E. Church." Nowadays the name evokes no memory, nor does it identify the man.

CHAPTER VII

The Denmark Vesey Affair

ON THURSDAY, JULY 2, 1822, A BOY OF ELEVEN CLIMBED the balcony of his house on the corner of Hutson and King streets and watched, away in the distance, the bodies of six men swinging on the Lines, the city's boundary. One of them, he was told, was a free man of color, like Abraham who ran the blacksmith's shop on Boundary Street. Only this man had been a carpenter, and he had plotted with the slaves to kill all the white people in their beds, set the city on fire and sail away to an island called Santo Domingo where black men ruled the land.[1]

Meanwhile, in the stifling heat of a closed courtroom, the dead free black went down in history, as the court of magistrates and freeholders unfolded a spine-chilling tale known to history as the Denmark Vesey uprising. One hundred and twenty-six terrified witnesses quailed before the law, stammered, denied, pleaded, accused and eventually contributed to the evidence that justice demanded. They told of a plot of four years' patience; of the Bible quoted and distorted, of a subversive church, of a fraternal

[1] Elizabeth B. Pharo, ed., *Reminiscences of William Hasell Wilson (1811–1902)* (Philadelphia, 1937), pp. 6–10.

meal of parched corn and groundnuts; of a "little man
. . . who can't be killed, shot or caught"; of promised aid
from England, the islands and a band of Frenchmen a
hundred strong; of a list of nine thousand men and of
powder and shot; and finally of a breakneck ride to the
country, to bring in the field hands in a last-minute attempt to avert the disaster of discovery. When the court
adjourned, 35 of the 131 accused had been sentenced to
death and 37 more to transportation outside the limits of
the state.[2] Two slaves whose information had led to the
discovery of the plot were granted their freedom and an
annuity of fifty dollars each. Two free blacks were re-
warded: George Pencil, whose advice had led one of the
slaves to report the existence of the plot; and a man named
Scott, who had aided the police in setting a trap for the
arrest of a white man known to have sympathized with the
convicted blacks.[3]

Although the uprising never took place, the existence
of a plot to overthrow the white regime has generally been
accepted by contemporaries and historians alike.[4] Writers
on both sides of the issue of slavery during this period
found a useful prop in the Denmark Vesey affair. To some

[2] Transportation presented something of a problem since South Carolina was not recognized as a sovereign state. The United States ambassador
in Altamina, Joel R. Poinsett, on behalf of his native state, investigated
the possibilities of selling the convicted slaves in South America, but to no
avail. Eventually, the slaves were transported to the rice fields of lower
Georgia and Alabama. Document B, Documents Relating to the Vesey
Uprising; Petition of the Executors of Joseph Yates, 1822, ibid.; Petition
of William Sims, 1822, ibid.; *Charleston Mercury*, Feb. 4, 1823; Orville J.
Victor, *A History of American Conspiracies: A Record of Treason, Insurrection, Rebellion etc. in the United States from 1760 to 1860*, p. 386.

[3] Document F, Documents Relating to the Vesey Uprising; Receipts of
Peter Desverney, 1827–57, ibid.; Petition of Peter Desverney, a free person of color, for an increase of the annual bounty conferred upon him,
1837, ibid.; *City Gazette* (Charleston), Dec. 25, 1822.

[4] The conclusions of the Court of Magistrates and Freeholders were
seriously challenged for the first time, in 1964, by Richard C. Wade in an
article, "The Vesey Plot: A Reconsideration," pp. 143–61.

it pointedly revealed the unity of the black race in the face of the oppressive slave system. Denmark Vesey thus took on the semblance of a martyr. In the view of others, the abortive insurrection underscored the need for the rigid control of race relations. Vesey was thus no mere villain of the piece; he was rather the symbol of the sable terror.[5] These conclusions were based on the three major printed sources available: the account published by James Hamilton, Jr., intendant of Charleston; Gov. Thomas Bennett's message to the legislature in 1822; and the report issued by Lionel Kennedy and Thomas Parker, examining magistrates in the Vesey trials. The Kennedy-Parker report is perhaps the fullest of the three accounts. Kennedy and Parker recorded the evidence, sifted the facts and drew their conclusions, but the Report does not quite tally with the manuscript records of the trials. It omits a good deal of evidence and makes significant alterations in the statements of witnesses; and more curiously, it includes confessions not recorded in the trials. The conclusion which the report makes inevitable thus becomes dubious, and a reexamination of the evidence opens it to challenge.[6]

The first inkling the authorities had of the contemplated uprising came on the thirtieth of May, when a slave reported a conversation he had overheard on one of the wharves. Little credence was paid to him, but as a measure

[5] Carter G. Woodson, *The Negro in Our History* (Washington, D.C., 1927), p. 180; Dwight L. Dumond, *Antislavery: The Crusade for Freedom in America* (Ann Arbor, 1961), p. 114; John Hope Franklin, *From Slavery to Freedom*, p. 210; Herbert Aptheker, *American Negro Slave Revolts* (New York, 1943), p. 270; John Lofton, *Insurrection in South Carolina: the Turbulent World of Denmark Vesey;* Ulrich B. Phillips, "The Slave Labor Problem in the Charleston District," pp. 429–30.

[6] Lionel H. Kennedy and Thomas Parker, *An Official Report of the Trials of Sundry Negroes Charged With an Attempt to Raise An Insurrection in the State of South Carolina;* James Hamilton, Jr., *An Account of the Late Intended Insurrection Among a Portion of the Blacks of this City; Niles Register;* Documents Relating to the Vesey Uprising.

of precaution William Paul, one of the slaves identified by the informer, was arrested and placed in solitary confinement in "the black hole of the Workshop." A week passed and no further light was thrown on the subject. Then Paul, "beginning to fear that he would soon be led forth to the scaffold, for summary execution, confessed that he had for sometime known of the plot, that it was very extensive, embracing an indiscriminate massacre of the whites. . . ." The details he supplied defy the imagination. Even the governor admitted that Paul "so amplified the circumstances, that the utmost credulity was requisite to the belief of his tale."[7] It was clearly the fanciful story of a desperate man. The matter was dismissed. Then, on the fourteenth of June, two weeks after Paul's arrest, a slaveholder reported a rumored plot within the African church, scheduled to take place on the night of the sixteenth. The militia was alerted, the night of the sixteenth came and passed, and no insurrection took place. But on the eighteenth of June ten blacks were arrested, among them Denmark Vesey, a free black class leader in the African church. Events had begun to move.[8]

Vesey, who had been silent throughout his trial, was convicted on the confession of one of the suspects arrested with him. The actual evidence against him was unfolded after his execution, when many more blacks had been arrested and put on trial. There was general agreement as to the leaders of the plot, many of whom were class leaders and all of whom were acknowledged as leaders in the black community. Beyond this the plot divided into a labyrinth

[7] Kennedy and Parker, *Report*, pp. 52–53; Narrative of the investigation of the Vesey Plot, Executive Department, Charleston, Aug. 10, 1822, Document A, Documents Relating to the Vesey Uprising.

[8] Narrative of the investigation of the Vesey Plot, Executive Department, Charleston, Aug. 10, 1822, Document A, Documents Relating to the Vesey Uprising.

of subplots as individual witnesses recorded the details of
the master plot told to them by its leaders or overheard in
conversations among the slaves. Particularly confusing was
the date: some spoke of the sixteenth of June, others of
the Fourth of July, others of the sixth of July; all agreed
that the time set was midnight, an auspicious hour for
subterranean enterprises. The plan was evidently im-
mature, however, for none of the leaders of the plot could
outline a coherent plan of action. The details developed,
rather, in the little circles of slaves who surreptitiously
discussed the arrests, the trials, the evidence thus far recorded and ultimately came to court to tell what they
knew.[9] As the plot developed in court it assumed new
proportions. Witnesses testified to the weapons accumulated over four years, they told of kegs of powder stored on
a farm, stealthy raids on the arsenal and pikes sharpened
in preparation for the test. The weapons were recovered
and produced in court—twelve poles found on a farm, "a
quantity of slow match, supposed to have been stolen out
of the Arsenal . . . found on one of the wharves, and
some musket balls accidentally discovered under water in
one of the docks"—this the materiel for an army nine
thousand strong.[10]

The trial revolved around the evidence of three witnesses for the state: Monday Gell, Harry Haig and Charles
Drayton. All three had been sentenced to death on the
evidence of an unidentified slave, and immediately after
the sentence had been pronounced the three had been left
together in a common ward until separate cells could be
provided for them. That same night, Drayton sent for the
intendant, "in a state of the most lamentable depression

[9] Documents A, B, Documents Relating to the Vesey Uprising; Kennedy
and Parker, *Report*, p. 25.

[10] Document B, Documents Relating to the Vesey Uprising; Kennedy
and Parker, *Report*, p. 39.

and panic, and he seemed prepared to make the most ample declarations from the fear of death." Observing the efficacy of this treatment, the court decided to continue it. Thereafter the three prisoners were deliberately left together, and, with the added inducement of a pardon from the governor, they were soon ready to disclose all the details of the plot. It was Monday Gell who declared Denmark Vesey, now dead, to be the ringleader of the abortive uprising; as the governor later observed, all three seemed to have predicated their chances of acquittal on the number of convictions they could instigate. The net grew wider; by a process of implication and counterimplication more blacks were arrested. The suspects soon totaled 131.[11]

The procedure of the trial is not completely recorded in either the report or the manuscript record; the manuscript, however, contains fragments of the examination and cross-examination of witnesses. The following account, for instance, reveals a great deal about the nature of the evidence.

Trial of Caesar, slave of Mrs. Smith—Mr. McDow attended for Mrs. Smith.
John Enslow examined—"The prisoner is engaged [in the rebellion] and confessed it to me. I have seen him often at Monday's. He belongs to the African Church and is a native of Africa and came here as a boy." [Witness seeing Mr. McDow:] "He told me sometimes in the street he was engaged. . . ."[12]

Monday Gell also declared that Caesar, "who was zealous as any," was on his list (which was never produced in

[11] Kennedy and Parker, *Report,* pp. 57–58; Further confession of Monday Gell, Documents B and F, Documents Relating to the Vesey Uprising; Governor's Message to the Senate, No. 2, Nov. 28, 1822, in Messages of the Governors of South Carolina to the Legislature.
[12] Trial of Caesar, Document B, Documents Relating to the Vesey Uprising.

court), but on cross-examination by McDow "he [Gell] answered none of the questions."[13] Caesar was eventually convicted on the evidence recorded.

According to the Kennedy-Parker report, the court established some rules of justice which it maintained throughout the trial. No slave was to be tried in secret, the accused was to be confronted with the witnesses against him, and the testimony of one witness alone was not to lead to the conviction of the accused. The court appears to have discarded these principles with the same abandon with which it convicted the blacks indicted before it. Testimony was frequently received in secret and the witnesses' identity never disclosed. Agrippa Perry, whose evidence refuting the much-publicized ride to the country was corroborated by his master, was sentenced to transportation on the sole evidence of a fellow slave, Perault Strohecker.[14] The basis of the convictions was twofold. Sentenced to death were those who, in the words of the court, had "exhibited peculiar energy and activity," while "those who did little (if any more) than yield their acquiescence to the proposal to enter the plot" were sentenced to transportation. The court did not define the particular object of this "peculiar energy and activity." On the general assumption that it was directed toward the overthrow of the state, thirty-five blacks were sentenced to die.[15]

Denmark Vesey's role in the affair has remained something of a mystery. What we do know of him is drawn chiefly from the court's report, and from the indications of individual witnesses that he was a rather forbidding per-

[13] Ibid.

[14] Kennedy and Parker, *Report*, p. viii; Evidence of "Y," Document B, Documents Relating to the Vesey Uprising; Governor's Message, ibid.; Petition of Ann Drayton Perry, November 1822, ibid.

[15] Court of Magistrates and Freeholders to Governor Bennett, July 24, 1822, Document F, Documents Relating to the Vesey Uprising.

sonality, respected but not very well liked in the black community. Carried to Santo Domingo as a boy, he had been returned to the slave trader, Capt. Joseph Vesey, on the grounds that he was physically unsound and subject to epilepsy. Captain Vesey apparently had no cause to regret the transaction, for the slave Denmark served him faithfully for twenty years. In 1800 he drew a prize in a lottery, with which he bought his freedom and set himself up as a carpenter in Charleston. The court rather fancifully recorded from sources outside the courtroom that "His temper was impetuous and domineering in the extreme, qualifying him for the despotic rule, of which he was ambitious. All his passions were ungovernable and savage, and to his numerous wives and children, he displayed the haughty and capricious cruelty of an Eastern Bashaw." From conjecturing his character the court went on to conjecture his role in the plot. "Vesey being a free man encountered none of those obstacles which would have been in the way of a slave; his time was at his own disposal, and he could go wherever he pleased without interruption; qualifications and advantages absolutely necessary for the Chief in a Conspiracy."[16] The conclusion so simply arrived at might well have been made independently of the evidence recorded. Vesey had been a free black, a pernicious influence on the slaves; he may have lacked the motive, but he had had the opportunity; and he had been a class leader in the African church.

The city authorities had been inclined to disbelieve the earliest information of a plot to overthrow the white order. It was not until the plot had been linked to the recently established African Methodist Episcopal church that the authorities became convinced of the possibility of a plot. The growth of an independent African church had been

16 Kennedy and Parker, *Report*, pp. 27–28.

regarded from the outset as a threat to the very foundations of slavery. Not only did the church aspire to interpret the Bible for itself, but it had maintained strong ties with its parent church in Philadelphia, the high seat of abolitionism. Members of the church in Charleston attended annual conferences in Philadelphia, invited Northern ministers to preach at meetings and drew large numbers of blacks to the organization, leaving a very noticeable gap in the memberships of the white churches. Several attempts had been made to obstruct the African meetings by large-scale arrests and imprisonments for disturbing the peace. In 1820, on the heels of the Missouri controversy, the charge of abolitionism had been directed against the church but had not been proved.[17] Various efforts to destroy the institution had failed. The law of 1800, which had imposed limitations on blacks' worship, could not be invoked against it, for it was widely admitted that the law was little more than a dead letter. Furthermore, the church was a legally constituted body, and the legislature would need stronger justification than the charge of disturbance to revoke the charter it had granted.

Implication in the threat of a slave insurrection presented an airtight case against the church. South Carolinians lived under the constant shadow of the successful slave rebellion in Santo Domingo. In 1794 the state had actively assisted the marooned white government, and, when all else had failed, had provided a haven for the displaced French refugees. But strong suspicions had always been entertained against the more liberal Frenchmen, and more particularly against the blacks the French had brought with them. The letters of "Rusticus" voiced the fears of the majority in the state when he declared that "an excess of humanity has led us to be totally blind to

[17] See Chapter VI.

our interests and that mindful alone of their situation, we have forgot the dangers of our own. . . . From the moment we admitted the St. Domingo Negroes into our own Country, security from that source became daily more precarious."[18]

The earliest evidence recorded in the trials made no allusions to the African church. On cross-examination, however, many witnesses admitted to membership in the organization, and thereafter the connection was established with increasing rapidity. The indicted slaves were more than willing to supply the evidence their masters required. Reexamined, William Paul and Bacchus Hammett declared that the plot had originated in 1818, when the African church had begun to worship in the building at Hampstead. As the trial's new direction was discussed outside the courtroom, more evidence piled up. A slave came forward and confessed that "One of Col. Cross' wenches about the house . . . told me that Joseph the former cook of Col. Cross said that Morris Brown swore them on the Bible never to divulge the secret, even if they suffered death."[19] From hearsay evidence to direct participation, the court was able to build up a case. It pointed out that dissatisfaction among the colored population had originated with the establishment of an independent church, "that inflammatory and insurrectionary doctrines

[18] *Massachusetts Spy or Worcester Gazette*, Dec. 20, 1797; Affidavit of Captain Paul, 1792, in Correspondence of the Governor of South Carolina with the French Assembly in St. Domingo, 1791–1793; President of the colonial assembly of the French section of St. Domingue to members of the South Carolina legislature, Aug. 26, 1791, M. Polony to Congress of South Carolina, ybre 1791, ibid.; Charles Pinckney to assembly at St. Domingue, 1791, ibid.; Accounts of the Benevolent Society to the Corporation of Charleston for sums paid for the reception of the poor French from Santo Domingo, ibid.; Letters of "Rusticus," 1794.

[19] Evidence of John Enslow, Re-examination of William Paul, Further confession of Bacchus, Confession of William Colcock's slave to Thomas C. Jervey, in Document B, Documents Relating to the Vesey Uprising.

. . . were inculcated at these meetings"; and it even recalled that Denmark Vesey's conduct and language had
changed since the establishment of the church four years
before. "Is it to be wondered at," the court concluded,
"that, under all the foregoing circumstances, an attempt to
create an insurrection should be contemplated."[20]

The court appears to have been impelled by a strong
sense of inevitability, or, perhaps, by a stronger appreciation of logic. The creation of an independent church
smacked strongly of revolt. Its revolutionary teachings and
meetings contributed to making it, as Intendant James
Hamilton described it, "a hot-bed in which the germ might
well be expected to spring into life and vigor." Given the
circumstances and conditions for revolt it was impossible
that a revolt should not germinate. The sheer force of the
syllogism revealed the African church as the source of the
insurrection. It was less easy, however, to impugn the motives of its founder, Morris Brown, a man of some reputation among both the black and white populations. But a
few months after the court had adjourned he was charged
with having left the state and reentered it in violation of
the Act of 1820; found guilty, he was ordered to leave the
state within fifteen days. All that remained of the church
—its building in Hampstead—was destroyed shortly thereafter by order of the city authorities.[21]

The court's conclusions found wide acceptance among
the white population, chiefly among the white churches,
which had suffered some loss of membership when the
African church had been established. A spokesman for the
Episcopal church agreed that revolt was inevitable when
religious instruction was "left to the crude undigested

---

[20] Kennedy and Parker, *Report*, p. 23.

[21] Hamilton, *An Account of the Late Intended Insurrection*, p. 30; Kennedy and Parker, *Report*, p. 23; *City Gazette* (Charleston), Aug. 10,
1822; F. A. Mood, *Methodism in Charleston*, p. 133.

ideas of illiterate black class-leaders." The Baptist church, fearing perhaps that its own fundamentalist teachings would be brought into question, hinted strongly at the "intimate connection" that the African church had with "a similar body of men in a Northern City, among whom the supposed right to emancipation is strenuously advocated." Among the ministers of the Gospel, only the Reverend John B. Adger questioned the church's connection with the attempted insurrection. "[T]he people of Charleston very naturally were under very great excitement" he recalled in 1889, "and it was almost inevitable that their suspicions should attach to that poor African church." But the clergyman was unshaken in his belief that an insurrection had been planned, not by religious fanatics, as the court had maintained, but by materially minded men in quest of "blood and booty."[22]

Throughout the trials, Gov. Thomas Bennett maintained a detached and somewhat skeptical view of the whole affair. When one of his slaves had seemed in danger of implication, the governor, confident of the man's innocence, had sent him to the authorities to have him cleared of suspicion. Eventually, the slave and two others in the governor's household were convicted and hanged. It is possible that the governor's skepticism derived from a subjective interest in the trials, but Bennett had long evinced a liberal attitude toward the black. A year earlier, he had recommended reforms in the trials of blacks as "urgent claims to the justice, humanity and prompt attention of the Legislature." The Vesey trials confirmed his

[22] A South Carolinian [Frederick Dalcho?], *Practical Considerations Founded on the Scriptures Relative to the Slave Population of South Carolina*, p. 33; Richard Furman, *Exposition of the Views of the Baptists Relative to the Colored Population of the United States in a Communication to the Governor of South Carolina*, p. 17; John B. Adger, *My Life and Times, 1810–1899*, pp. 54–55.

conclusions. Convinced of the lack of evidence to support the convictions, the governor dissented strongly from the conclusions of the court and the methods by which they were reached.[23] In June of the same year, while the trials were in progress, an unsigned "Communication" in the *Charleston Courier* also questioned the fairness of the trials. Its author was William Johnson, a justice of the U.S. Supreme Court. Both Bennett and Johnson, however, were evidently an isolated minority. Bennett was forced to abandon hope of reelection in 1822, and Johnson's comment aroused such a furore that he was obliged to issue an explanation asserting his attachment to the institutions of the state.[24]

The slaveholders, who had perhaps the most to fear from an uprising, had cooperated willingly in the trials, many of them voluntarily committing their slaves if they entertained the slightest doubts about them. Owners whose slaves were sentenced to death received ample compensation, for the state provided that the value of any slave executed should be paid to his owner. Owners of slaves who had merely "acquiesced" in the plot and were subsequently sentenced to transportation found themselves in a quandary. Not only were they denied compensation, but the responsibility of transporting the convicts also fell on them; meanwhile they had to pay for the maintenance of the slave in the city's workhouse. Small wonder, then, that many slaveholders began to entertain second thoughts about the insurrection. A spate of petitions reached the legislature before the year was out.

[23] Governor's Message to the Legislature, Nov. 29, 1821, in Messages of the Governors of South Carolina to the Legislature; Governor's Message No. 2, 1822, ibid.; Thomas Bennett to the Court of Magistrates and Freeholders, July 25, 1822, Document F, Documents Relating to the Vesey Uprising; see also Document A, ibid.

[24] *Charleston Courier*, June 21, 29, 1822; Theodore D. Jervey, *Robert Y. Hayne and His Times*, pp. 132–33.

William Sims asserted that his convicted slave Scipio had "always been an Orderly and honest Negro"; Mrs. Ann Drayton Perry affirmed the innocence of her slave Agrippa and decried the justice which demanded that "an unfortunate fellow creature . . . [be] torn from his children and family."[25] It seemed that both slaveholders and magistrates had acted hastily. Casual expressions of discontent had been blown up into a plot; leaders of the black community naturally had become instigators of the plot; and the African church had been a well-chosen scapegoat.

Nevertheless, the trials had generated a very real fear among South Carolinians, and it was difficult to shake off the impact of the events of that summer. The Denmark Vesey affair convinced the white population that the ever-present fear of slave uprisings was not unjustified. In its wake there was unearthed a series of threatened uprisings —in Beaufort, in Georgetown and in other urban areas where the blacks were most heavily concentrated. The town council of Georgetown appears to have had a field day rounding up culprits for execution, evidently a welcome change from its sedentary occupation. The attending judicial ceremony mounted up an expenditure of $1,669.32, of which $140.00 was spent in furnishing refreshments for the guard, $367.20 on liquor for eleven men, and $1.00 for clearing away the weeds in the magazine.[26] Once the general excitement had died down, however, idle pastimes gave way to serious introspection. The

[25] Petition of Mrs. Jane Thompson, 1822, Petition of William Sims, Petition of Mrs. Ann Drayton Perry, 1822, in Petitions Relating to Slavery.

[26] *Charleston Mercury*, Sept. 24, 1822; Petition of Francis Kinloch for compensation for slave "Mood" executed for plotting an insurrection in Georgetown, in Petitions Relating to Slavery; Petition of Hannah Tait, ibid.; Petition of William Vaught, Nov. 20, 1829, ibid.; Petition of the Town Council of Georgetown, 1829, in Report of Committees of the South Carolina Legislature.

merest hint of an insurrection in South Carolina indicated that all was not well within the state. On the surface it called into question the efficacy of that highly developed police system, the patrol. But beneath lurked the possibility that the institution of slavery was not as stable as it seemed.

Perhaps it was this realization that led Governor Bennett to insist repeatedly that a successful rebellion could not take place in the state because "the liberal and enlightened humanity of our Fellow-Citizens produce many attachments that operate as checks on the spirit of insubordination."[27] The governor's assertion was hardly reassuring. Yet to concede that the disturbances arose from conditions within the state would be to entail for it dire consequences. Bennett feared that "the reputation of the State must suffer abroad, and a rapid deterioration of property occur within. . . ."[28] The governor, the court and the legislature thus embarked on a solution that was far more feasible—a search for external causes.

While the trial of the blacks was in progress, four white men stood arraigned before the regular courts on the charge of having incited the slaves to insurrection. All four were sentenced to long terms of imprisonment, heavy fines and security for future good behavior. Three were foreigners—a Scot, a Spaniard and a German. The Spaniard had had the misfortune to declare, in a conversation overheard by white witnesses, that he disliked everything in Charleston save the blacks and the sailors; the German had announced that he thought the indicted blacks were innocent; and the Scot had fallen into a trap laid for him by the police, when, in a fit of drunken extravagance, he

[27] Governor's Message, 1822, in Messages of the Governors of South Carolina to the Legislature.

[28] Document A, Documents Relating to the Vesey Uprising.

had offered assistance to a free black informer in a scheme to rescue the convicted blacks.[29] Foreigners had in fact always shown an irritating irreverence for the state's peculiar institution, and Charleston's proximity to the French West Indies had inevitably attracted the heirs of the French Revolution, whose experiment in fraternity there had been deferred by black uprisings. Charleston, however, was ever alert to the dangers of the subversive foreign element. In 1804, James Negrin, a Swiss immigrant of ten years' residence, had published a *Life of Toussaint* (L'Ouverture) which had been well received and had even sold some copies in Charleston. The city authorities, how-ever, had soon discovered that it was "intended to excite domestic insurrection." Negrin had been imprisoned on the charge, his property and printing press had been sold by his landlord to cover his rent, and he had come out of prison eight months later not only persona non grata but also a pauper.[30] It was, after all, a time-honored apothegm that behind every threat to native security there lurked an alien.

Unlike her sister states to the north, Virginia and North Carolina, South Carolina's ranks had always been firmly closed to antislavery sentiment. With very few exceptions, critics of the institution in the state drifted toward the American Colonization Society, which enjoyed wide and varied support.[31] Abolitionism had never been tolerated whether its roots were internal or external. Overtures from the earliest groups, organized in Philadelphia, had been rejected out of hand, and, as early as 1800, suspicions

[29] Kennedy and Parker, *Report*, Appendix.
[30] Petition of James Negrin, n.d., in Reports of Committees of the South Carolina Legislature.
[31] Petition of inhabitants of St. Luke's Parish, in Petitions Relating to Slavery; Jervey, *Hayne and His Times*, pp. 67, 205, 207-9; this subject is discussed further in Chapter IX.

of abolitionist tendencies therein had prompted the legislature to outlaw the religious meetings of blacks. The Denmark Vesey affair coincided with a renewed campaign against abolitionists, which followed in the wake of the Missouri controversy.[32] It was inevitable that the Vesey affair and the war against abolitionists should be connected. Before the year was out a variety of pamphlets under a variety of pseudonyms had flooded the market, all of which undertook to analyze the circumstances that had threatened the security of the white population. All arrived, by different methods, at the same conclusion: the institution of slavery was fundamentally stable; the threat came rather from the "indiscreet zeal in favor of universal liberty" shown by Northern states and unwarranted attempts from without to interfere with the domestic tranquillity of the state. Legislation composed only half the battle; what was needed was public vigilance. When Massachusetts' legal representative came down to South Carolina to test the Negro Seamen's Act the following year, he was literally run out of the state.[33]

The most obvious scapegoat, of course, lay within the state—the free black, that constant challenge to the assumptions on which the state's race relations were founded. His role in every slave insurrection, whether real or anticipated, was predetermined. The Denmark Vesey affair was little more than a reproduction of a historical drama, staged in Charleston in 1775, in 1797 and in 1800, and reenacted in the districts on innumerable, though less-

[32] Memorial of sundry delegates in convention assembled in the city of Philadelphia for the abolition of slavery, Jan. 7, 1795, in Petitions Relating to Slavery; see also Chapter VI.

[33] Achates [Thomas Pinckney?], *Reflections Occasioned by the Late Disturbances in Charleston*, pp. 6–7; Furman, *Exposition*, p. 16; [Robert J. Turnbull and Isaac Holmes] *Caroliniensis* (Charleston, n.d.) ; *Charleston Mercury*, Aug. 19, 20, 1822; Lofton, *Insurrection in South Carolina*, p. 210.

publicized occasions. In 1775, when feeling ran high against the British, and South Carolinians themselves were contemplating insurrection against the established government, a black plot was discovered and a wealthy free black pilot hanged along with several of his accomplices. According to the governor, Lord William Campbell, the plot was no more than a discussion of the "imprudent conversations" overheard by the slaves in the parlors of their white masters. Several slaves were arrested, and "terrified at the recollection of former cruelties were easily induced to accuse themselves and others to escape punishment." The governor was convinced of the innocence of the free black pilot, whom he thought was a scapegoat and the supposed interests of internal security in no way assuaged his conscience. "I could not save him my Lord," he wrote to Dartmouth, Secretary of State for the American Department. "The very reflection harrows my soul. I have only the comfort to think I left no means untried to preserve him."[34]

The number of free blacks involved in the Denmark Vesey trials was remarkably small,[35] but the leadership ascribed to Vesey inescapably linked the free black with the uprising. The trials were followed by a public outcry against their number. A memorial to the legislature insisted that the source of the revolt lay in the situation of urban Charleston, which brought the slave into close contact with the free black. The free black's degraded status was an incentive for him to rebel; at the same time his

[34] British Public Record Office Transcripts (America and the West Indies), Vol. 35, pp. 184–90, 191–205.

[35] Eleven free blacks were indicted; eight of them were acquitted, two were sentenced to transportation, and one was hanged. Memorial of the city council praying remuneration for expenses incurred in the apprehension of the conspirators in the late intended insurrection, in Documents Relating to the Denmark Vesey Uprising, 1822.

privileges encouraged the slaves to rebel. Free black plantations were the seedbeds in which the plots inevitably germinated. The memorialists found that the only solution lay in the withdrawal of blacks' property rights.[36] It was even suggested by some that all free blacks be expelled from the state. Impatient of the dilatory shortcomings of the regular government, citizens convened a public meeting to consider changes in the laws relating to free blacks and formed vigilante associations to ensure the enforcement of laws already on the statute books.[37]

The response to this outcry was curiously mild. The governor's message to the legislature suggested that the threat to the security of slavery came not from the local free blacks, who had accepted their freedom under the definition of the state's laws, but from the large numbers of free black immigrants who had sought refuge from the repressive laws of neighboring states. He suggested, accordingly, that recent immigrants be expelled and the state's frontiers closed to future black immigrants. The solution clearly lay in keeping the number of free blacks low, in order to ensure effective control. Both the city council and the legislature appear to have agreed with him; legislation following the Vesey affair barely went beyond the governor's proposals. The immigration of free blacks had already been prohibited by the Act of 1820. In 1822 the legislature imposed a tax on free blacks of less than five years domicile, restricted travel beyond the state and revived the law which made guardians compulsory for free blacks over fifteen years of age. And, as a concession to public fears, it recommended an appropriation

[36] *Charleston Mercury*, Nov. 30, 1822; *City Gazette* (Charleston), Dec. 4, 1822.

[37] *Charleston Courier*, Nov. 13, 1822, Jan. 31, 1823; *Charleston Mercury*, Aug. 19, 20, 1822.

of $100,000 for the construction of a citadel in the city of Charleston.[38]

The Negro Seamen's Act, which was passed shortly after, was not a new device produced in the excitement following the Vesey trials. It received much publicity, however, because roughshod enforcement of the act intensified sectional tensions and embarrassed the United States government in its relations with foreign nations. The manner of enforcement might itself have derived from the sectional issue, but that subject is not within the purview of this study.[39] A similar law had been on the statute books for twenty-eight years. In 1800 a notice in the *Charleston City Gazette* had reminded masters of vessels to report any persons of color they had brought into the state and assume written responsibility for them.[40] The Seamen's Act merely revived a law that had attracted little attention until the Denmark Vesey uprising reminded citizens of its feasibility. Vesey had been the slave of a sea captain, had seemingly been in contact with blacks from Santo Domingo and had frequented the wharves. The subsequent furore over the act enhanced the legislature's role as the custodian of the state's security. It also deflected the excitement which the threatened uprising had generated.

This legislative constraint is all the more remarkable in the context of the restrictions imposed on free blacks only two years earlier. But the Vesey "uprising" had served

[38] Governor's Message, 1822, in Messages of the Governors of South Carolina to the Legislature; Memorial of the city council of Charleston to the Senate, n.d., in Reports of Committees of the South Carolina Legislature; David. J. McCord, ed., *The Statutes At Large of South Carolina*, VII, pp. 461–62, hereafter referred to as *Statutes at Large; Charleston Mercury*, Dec. 11, 18, 1822.

[39] The issue is discussed comprehensively in the latter half of Lofton's *Insurrection in South Carolina*.

[40] *Statutes At Large*, VII, pp. 433, 463–66; *City Gazette* (Charleston), June 30, 1800.

some purpose. The African church had been demolished, its leaders exiled, the errant blacks who had left the white churches restored to the fold, and the plot's chief participants hanged. The Denmark Vesey affair undoubtedly made a strong impact on the national scene; but its essence lay, of course, in the plot. It was, as Shakespeare might have expressed it, "A good plot, good friends and full of expectation; an excellent plot. . . ." It was ironic, however, that plotter and victim should reverse their roles.

CHAPTER VIII

Freedom's Crisis

THE DENMARK VESEY AFFAIR SERVED IN MANY WAYS TO diagnose the state's problem regarding the free black. On the one hand, the implication of free blacks in the "uprising," indeed, the very fact that its leader was a free black, suggested that it was expedient to enslave all blacks in the interests of security. On the other hand, free blacks had assisted in informing the authorities and arresting the culprits. If the freeman's allegiance could be secured, he might conceivably constitute a buffer between the master class and the slaves.

A debate on options was maintained in South Carolina throughout the antebellum period. The popular view, as expressed in numerous petitions and grand jury presentments, was strongly unfavorable to the free colored population. Free blacks were a menace to the institution of slavery: they harbored runaway slaves, they enticed well-bred house slaves into grogshops and brothels, they were insubordinate and their freedom bred discontent among the usually docile slave population. This hostility was strongest among rural whites, who were outnumbered by the blacks. Preoccupied with the immediate concerns of economic and social security, they saw no necessity for tolerating an anomaly in the established system of race relations. They might well have agreed with the laconic Kentucky yeoman whom James Stirling met on his travels: "I like a nigger," said he, "but I hate a damned free nigger."[1]

The free black's survival outside the slave system challenged the very foundations of that institution. It was generally maintained that slavery was a boon to the black man, that the African race could not hold its own in a predominantly white civilization, and that slavery gave the black protection, trained him in his skills, Christianized him and controlled his social behavior. Released from this straitjacket the black, it was held, would revert to his original state and disqualify himself for existence in white civilization. There was, in short, no option beyond slavery for the black in white society. The small group of independent free black artisans, farmers and *rentiers* gave the lie to this myth. Rather than confront the reality, white slaveholders felt an increasing need to assert the rationale for slavery, and the need expressed itself in frequent attempts to destroy the evidence which so strongly undermined that rationale. A petition from Abbeville District reveals the problem in all its implications:

We consider them [free blacks] the most degraded people that live in a civilized community. We of the South understand the Negro character. We know that naturally they are indolent, lazy, improvident, destitute of forethought, and totally incapable of self-government. With such proclivities they are incapable of supporting themselves and should have someone to arouse their dormant energies and direct their labor. But apart from themselves, they have decidedly a demoralizing

[1] James Stirling, *Letters from the Slave States*, pp. 243–44.

effect upon our slave-population. . . . We regard their condition socially and politically as most deplorable and consider them proper subjects of legislative action. We would therefore humbly prey that you would enact some form for their relief, by placing them in a happy state of bondage, the place where God designed the African race to be—If your honorable body is not disposed to grant this boon to these unfortunate people. Then we pray you to appropriate a fund and have them removed to Liberia and thus relieve the State of their contaminating influence.[2]

Like many others of its kind, this petition was rejected out of hand by the state legislature. The government of South Carolina tended, on the whole, to be lenient toward the free black. Admittedly, it was not disposed to make any concessions to free blacks in the state, but it resisted with equal resolution the attempts of numerous groups to enslave them or deprive them of the meager rights they enjoyed.

More in the interests of statecraft perhaps than of humanity, the government upheld the independence of the free black. Free blacks supported the state by taxation, both directly and indirectly, and their economic activities contributed to its wealth. Particular encouragement was given to free black property holders, who had a vested interest in the state and who would be committed to maintaining the status quo. A stable class of free blacks, it was hoped, would provide an example for the slaves which the institution of slavery obviously lacked.[3] The whites' hopes

[2] Memorial of sundry citizens of Horry District, in Petitions Relating to Slavery; the petition of Charles M. Pelott and sundry citizens of Abbeville, ibid.

[3] Governor Thomas Bennett's Message No. 1, 1822, in Messages of the Governors of South Carolina to the Legislature. Prosperous free blacks reinforced such traditional values of white society as thrift, hard work and industry. The master could point to the success of the free black, especially if he had once been a slave, as an example of what such virtues

were partially fulfilled when emancipated slaves set out to amass a fortune based on slave labor. When free blacks like George Pencil and an anonymous "free black," who merely identified himself as "one who is contented with his situation," informed the authorities of anticipated uprisings, the government was encouraged to regard its free colored population as a buffer between whites and slaves.[4]

The free black's fortunes, however, were always overshadowed by the great sense of insecurity which the peculiar institution had generated in the white population. The expanding cotton industry necessitated an expanding labor force, and every increase in its numbers made the slave population more unwieldy. Between 1800 and 1810 the black and white races were proportionate in numbers, but thereafter the black population increased at three times the rate of the white.[5] Outnumbered, the whites strengthened the patrol, built arsenals and citadels and made every effort to maintain a strict control over their slave population. But their fears persisted. Soon after the publication of the federal census of 1830, an alarmed grand jury in Georgetown called attention to the disproportionate racial distribution in the state and in Georgetown in particular, where a white population of 1,940 was pitted against 18,000 slaves and free persons of color. "It will not readily be credited," complained the grand jury, "that there are 1,700 slaves whose *10* masters are permanently (or rather for the last 12 months), absent from the district in which their property lies . . . and that among a black population of 15,000 located on the

could bring the slave, i.e., if he worked hard enough for the master he might be emancipated and perhaps provided for and launched on a similar career. The emphasis, of course, would be on cooperation with white society and an identification with its values.

4 "A Black" to His Excellency Governor Moultrie, Oct. 10, 1793, in Petitions Relating to Slavery.

5 Theodore D. Jervey, *Robert Y. Hayne and His Times*, p. 78.

tide swamp plantations . . . there remain during the summer months, no more than 40 proprietors."[6] South Carolinians readily recalled that the state's grand revolte noir, the Vesey affair, had been planned for the summer months. With even a muster of the entire white population the state could have offered little resistance to a massive black army.

The sable fear was intensified by the legacy South Carolina had inherited from Santo Domingo in 1794. When the successful slave uprising on that island threatened its white population, the port of Charleston, which had maintained a steady trade with the French West Indies, became the major haven for French refugees. They were warmly welcomed by the state. South Carolina had, in fact, made several attempts to assist the isolated white government in Santo Domingo. The welcome hardly extended, however, to the blacks, slave and free, who arrived with the white refugees. The fact that immigrant free blacks had rejected the island's black regime made little impression on white South Carolinians, who continued to regard the immigrant blacks with suspicion, as a contaminating influence on the local slaves. It seemed that in her zeal to welcome the victims, South Carolina had opened her doors to the culprits as well.[7]

Thereafter, every hint of discontent, every suspicion of a clandestine congregation of blacks sparked a reaction far

[6] Grand Jury Presentment, Georgetown District, Fall Term 1835.

[7] Charles Pinckney, Governor of South Caroliina to the assembly at Santo Domingo, 1791, in Correspondence of the Governor of South Carolina with the French Assembly at St. Domingo, 1791; President of the Colonial Assembly of St. Domingue to members of the South Carolina Legislature, Aug. 26, 1791, M. Polony to the Congress of South Carolina, 25th ybre, 1791, ibid.; Resolution of the House of Representatives for relief of refugees from Santo Domingo, 1793, ibid.; Accounts of the Benevolent Society to the Corporation of Charleston for sums paid for the reception of the poor French from Santo Domingo, Jan. 31, 1795, ibid.; Letters of "Rusticus," 1794.

in excess of the actual threat. The state never seemed to shake off the fear of infiltration from Santo Domingo. In 1795 the intendant of Charleston reported the arrest of "a very dangerous negro named Joukain, a Fellow who headed a parcel of colored people in Santo Domingo and engaged in a pitched Battle with the Whites." Much later, in 1802, the state sought federal assistance against some French blacks who were suspected of attempting to enter South Carolina through Northern ports.[8] Blacks who had already migrated were, of course, even more suspect. In 1797 four slaves from Santo Domingo were hanged for plotting an insurrection, following an inquiry which seems to anticipate the Vesey affair almost to the last detail.[9] The fear persisted even as late as 1816. It was inevitable that Denmark Vesey should look to Santo Domingo for assistance in his plot to massacre the whites and take over the city of Charleston.

The earliest restrictions on the free black were made in the wake of the Santo Domingo uprising. Concerned mainly with the threat from the island, the legislature in 1794 prohibited the immigration of free blacks from abroad, especially from the Bahamas and the West Indies islands. The act was renewed and revived in varying forms throughout the antebellum period, according to the dictates of the particular emergency.[10] Beyond this limitation on immigration, the Santo Domingo experience produced few repercussions on the free black population. Its mem-

[8] John Edwards, Intendant of Charleston, to Governor Vanderhorst, Nov. 3, 1795, in manuscripts of the South Carolina Archives Department; James Madison, Secretary of State, to Wade Hampton, Washington, Nov. 8, 1802, ibid.; Memorial of sundry citizens of Charleston, Dec. 11, 1797, ibid.; J. S. Richardson to Gov. D. R. Williams, Aug. 29, 1816, ibid.

[9] *Massachusetts Spy or Worcester Gazette*, Dec. 20, 1797.

[10] David J. McCord and Thomas Cooper, eds., *The Statutes At Large of South Carolina*, VII, pp. 433, 435–40, 444, 447, 449, 459–60, 461–67, 470–74, hereafter referred to as *Statutes At Large*.

bers were closely watched and liable to arrest on suspicion, but no attempt was made to deprive them of the rights they enjoyed.

In 1800 the legislature imposed some restrictions on manumission as a practical measure of regulation, but the act did very little to impede manumission and its repercussions on the free black population were negligible.[11] The same year, the reaction to the Methodist missionary effort among blacks and the charge of abolitionism within the church produced some restrictions on their religious assembly. Following an appeal from the Methodist ministers, however, the act was modified in 1803, giving added security to lawful religious assemblies.[12] These restrictions were remarkably mild by comparison with legislation of the same period in other states. In Maryland, for instance, the immigration of free blacks was absolutely prohibited and local free blacks were disfranchised, while restrictions on trade by free blacks cut off a basic source of livelihood. Georgia in 1810 made guardians compulsory for all its free colored population, and Tennessee and Louisiana imposed similar restrictions during the same period.[13] The general repression of free blacks in the rest of the South produced a vast influx of their numbers into South Carolina from neighboring states, particularly in the decade from 1810 to 1820.

In response perhaps to this increasing influx, the South Carolina legislature suddenly clamped down in 1820 with an omnibus act that made manumission subject to legislative consent, absolutely prohibited the immigration of free blacks, imposed restrictions on the egress and ingress of local free blacks and revived a law passed in 1794 re-

[11] See Chapter II.

[12] *Statutes At Large*, VII, pp. 440–43, 448–49. See also Chapter VI.

[13] Carter G. Woodson, *Free Negro Heads of Families in the United States in 1830*, pp. xxiv–xxv.

lating to masters of vessels who brought free blacks into
South Carolina. In addition, the act provided a penalty
on any free black or any white who "circulated or brought
within this State, any written or printed paper, with intent
to disturb the peace or security of the same in relation to
the slaves of the people of this State."[14]

The Missouri controversy of 1819–20 provoked an immediate reaction in South Carolina. As Thomas Jefferson
recognized, the issue provided the first outlet for deep-
seated sectional tensions. The debate penetrated every
stratum of society in the state, and the sectionalists mar-
shaled their forces early in preparation for the long struggle ahead. Members of the legislature, for example,
recognized the implicit victory in Missouri's refractory
constitution, which banned the entrance of free blacks into
the state, and enthusiastically endorsed it. The sectional
issue became the theme song of local politicians who developed what a contemporary described as "an inherited
passion to set forward the all-absorbing greatness of South
Carolina."[15] Unable to make headway against the federal
colossus, the champions of the state turned to attack the
enemy within.

Abolitionism had found little support in South Carolina
among either groups or individuals. The antislavery impulse emanated, rather, from the North, where feeble attempts were made to enlist the support of individual South
Carolinians. In 1795, delegates of abolition societies who
had assembled in convention at Philadelphia addressed
the South Carolina legislature on the subject of the international slave trade. Their petition was not even considered. Nor did the societies find support among individ-

[14] *Statutes At Large*, VII, pp. 459–60.
[15] Resolution of the Senate of South Carolina, Dec. 8, 1820, in Reports
of Committees of the South Carolina Legislature; F. C. Adams, *Manuel
Pereira*, p. 42.

uals. Groups of slaveholders frequently petitioned against the activities of Northern abolitionists in the state. When sectional tensions erupted in 1820, the abolitionists provided an easy target. Well before the advent of William Lloyd Garrison and *The Liberator,* South Carolina had closed her ranks to the thrust of abolitionism.[16]

The state's free blacks were caught in the line of fire. Independent, yet in close contact with the slaves, they might have been ideal agents for Northern abolitionism. Since they were free to leave the state and to reenter it, they might easily have conferred with abolitionists. In the past two years, since the establishment of the African church in Charleston, church leaders had in fact made frequent visits to general conferences in Philadelphia, the seat of abolitionism. It is significant that the only restraints imposed on free blacks within the state in 1820 related specifically to travel outside the state and to the distribution of antislavery literature. In December 1819 a bill had come up before the legislature proposing restraints on free blacks far in excess of the law passed the next year, but the legislature had not been interested in a campaign against free blacks per se and the bill had failed. In 1820, following Governor John Geddes' suggestion that it was "a duty to oppose at the threshold everything likely in its consequences to disturb our domestic tranquility," the legislature passed a law relating to free blacks which was closely modeled on the specific recommendations of the governor. The governor's message explicitly outlined a triple threat to domestic tranquillity—the debate on slavery provoked by the Missouri controversy, the "mischie-

[16] Memorial of sundry delegates in convention assembled in the city of Philadelphia for the abolition of slavery, Jan. 7, 1795, in Petitions Relating to Slavery; Petition of sundry citizens of Charleston, 1820, ibid. See also William B. Hesseltine, "Some New Aspects of the Pro-Slavery Argument," pp. 1–14.

vous effects" of abolitionism and the growing group of free blacks who were the catspaw of the abolitionists.[17] The common link, of course, was abolitionism. There was little that the single state of South Carolina could do against the movement throughout the nation, but the Act of 1820 effectively sealed off the state from its influence.

The direct impact of the act on the free black population was to restrict its expansion in numbers. The outright prohibition of black immigration and the virtual prohibition of manumission cut off the two major sources of its increase. In its positive defense of slavery, the state began to reflect on the negative impression a growing free black population must make on that institution. Yet South Carolina was willing to tolerate the existing anomaly. The sectional struggle had not yet reached its crisis; in 1822 Gov. Thomas Bennett still adhered to the view that a propertied free black class would sustain the stability of the state's institutions.[18]

Thus the Denmark Vesey affair did not produce the repression of free blacks that historians have attributed to its aftermath.[19] Beyond requiring guardians for all adult free blacks, tightening the laws on their egress and ingress and taxing recent free black immigrants, the state did little to hamper the free black's normal activities. On the other hand, a considerable effort was made to check the external forces which operated against the security of the slave system. Abolitionism was still a bugbear and it was necessary to isolate both the slave and the free black from external

[17] A bill to impose certain restrictions upon free persons of color, 1819, in Reports of Committees of the South Carolina Legislature; Message of Governor Geddes, No. 1, Nov. 27, 1820, in Messages of the Governors of South Carolina to the Legislature.

[18] Governor Bennett's Message No. 1, 1822, in Messages of the Governors of South Carolina to the Legislature.

[19] See Chapter VII.

contaminating influences. The law restricting the travel of free blacks was one such measure; the Negro Seamen's Act was another.

The Seamen's Act acquired a good deal of notoriety, due largely to its role in the struggle between North and South. The sectional pressure was applied in the state by the South Carolina Association, a vigilante organization dressed up in the gentility of a regular Charlestonian fraternity. The association was formed in 1823 "to facilitate the due enforcement of our laws in all cases connected with our colored population. . . . and as extra-official instruments in the preservation of the public peace." Boasting such names as Keating Simons, Gen. Thomas Pinckney and Joseph Manigault in its presidential and vice-presidential offices, the association actually came to be dominated by its secretary, Robert James Turnbull, and men of a similar political persuasion. Turnbull had been one of the freeholders before whom the Vesey trials were adjudicated, and his interest in their aftermath went well beyond the immediate security of the state. Greatly concerned with the sectional issue at the time of the Missouri controversy, Turnbull later went on to rouse the South to action against threatened federal consolidation in a pamphlet generally known as *The Crisis*.[20] Perhaps a belief in the advantages of attack in battle led him to direct the energies of the South Carolina Association into a stringent enforcement of the Negro Seamen's Act. The result was a sectional furore that continued well into the next decade. The free black found this deflection of the general alarm much to his advantage.

Admittedly South Carolina's white population con-

[20] Petition of the South Carolina Association, n.d., in Petitions Relating to Slavery; *Charleston Mercury*, July 26, 29, 1823; Robert James Turnbull, *The Crisis*.

tinued to be suspicious of free blacks and its fears took a toll on the free colored population in the way of a heightened patrol surveillance, greater demands for social subordination and the general need for the black to walk warily in the shadow of suspicion. The year following the Vesey affair, as Daniel Payne recalled, was a tense one for the denizens of the state. Still the trend was not one of overt repression. Two years after the Vesey affair, Gov. John L. Wilson was as insistent as Governor Bennett had been on the need for reform of the judicial procedure relating to blacks. Men on the order of Congressman (later Senator) Robert Y. Hayne and Justice John Belton O'Neall continued to plead for more moderation in the state's attitude toward its free black population.[21]

The free black in South Carolina enjoyed a long legislative respite that was denied his counterparts in the rest of the South. The decade of the 1830s witnessed a heightened campaign against the free black in many Southern states. Between 1831 and 1838, Maryland outlawed the navigation of vessels by free blacks and all assemblies of their number, and eventually provided for their removal to Liberia. Virginia, which had imposed restrictions on trading by free blacks in 1826, went on in 1832 to prohibit their ownership of slaves save by inheritance and in 1838 declared that all free blacks who left the state for educational purposes were debarred from returning. North Carolina and Tennessee explicitly outlawed marriages between blacks and whites, and Alabama in 1832, in one fell swoop, legislated free black immigrants and preachers out of existence.[22]

Public pressure was strong for the imposition of similar

21 Jervey, *Hayne and His Times*, pp. 180, 181–82; John Belton O'Neall, ed., *The Negro Law of South Carolina*, p. 35.
22 Woodson, *Free Negro Heads of Families*, pp. xxv, xxvii–xxx.

restrictions in South Carolina, but the legislature consistently rejected all petitions against free blacks. On one occasion the Committee on the Colored Population reported that it could not "perceive the policy or propriety of the harsh and severe legislation recommended for adoption against the free negroes of our State. . . . whilst they continue to conduct themselves with proper regard to the laws of the land and a proper appreciation and submission to the status assigned them, they would seem . . . to be more entitled to favor and encouragement than to oppression and expulsion from our borders."[23] Numerous bills were introduced in the legislature, but none passed, despite the fact that the Nat Turner insurrection in Virginia and the subsequent repression of free blacks in that state produced much anxiety and agitation in South Carolina.

The only legislation of note against free blacks in South Carolina during this period was an act which forbade their maintenance of schools. It did not specifically prohibit the education of free blacks, however, and there is reason to believe that its motive was personal rather than social. In 1829, Daniel Payne, a free black carpenter with a consuming scientific curiosity, had established a school in Charleston which soon catered to the leading white families in the city. Payne's curriculum, which excelled that of most of the white schools, included subjects like geography, botany, descriptive chemistry, descriptive astronomy and a course in practical zoology in which the class collected toads, snakes and baby alligators from neighboring plantations and dissected them in the privacy of the

[23] Report of the Committee on the Colored Population, Dec. 12, 1831, in Reports of Committees of the South Carolina Legislature; Grand Jury Presentment, Abbeville District, Fall Term, 1837; Report of the Committee on the Colored Population, in Reports of Committees of the South Carolina Legislature.

schoolroom. On one occasion, two white boys were out collecting snakes on the plantation of a Dr. Kennedy when they were accosted by the owner and his son, Lionel Kennedy, a representative in the House and one of the magistrates in the Vesey trials, and subjected to a detailed interrogation of their educational activities. The younger Kennedy's response is hardly gratifying. "Pa," he is said to have ejaculated, "Payne is playing hell in Charleston." The next day he introduced the bill which later became the Act of 1834.[24]

Apart from this attack, the free black emerged virtually unscathed from the decade of the 1830s. A few minor laws banning gaming between black and white and excluding free blacks from the occupations of clerk and salesman restrained their normal activities only slightly, though an act prohibiting manumission under any circumstances tended to isolate the group considerably.[25] Until 1860 no further legislation against the free colored population reached the statute books.

The free black's fortunes were reversed drastically, however, in the decade of the 1850s. As if in foreknowledge of the impending cataclysm, fears of black insurrection spread all over the South, from Clarksville, Tennessee, through Kentucky and Texas, all the way to Jacksonville, Florida, in the latter part of the decade, carrying in its wake a speedy white terror in the form of committees of vigilance. Throughout the South, free blacks were questioned, lynched and hanged; those who survived lost their freedom in most Southern States. In Maryland, Tennessee, Virginia, Louisiana, Texas and Arkansas legislation either facilitated voluntary enslavement or provided the free

[24] Daniel A. Payne, *Recollections of Seventy Years*, pp. 23, 25, 38; *Statutes At Large*, VII, p. 468.
[25] See Chapter II.

blacks with a Hobson's choice between exile and enslavement.[26]

South Carolina's immunity from insurrection during this period gave her free blacks no respite. Sectional tension ran high there also in the decade of the 1850s. As early as December 1850, the legislature anticipated secession and increased taxation by 50 percent with a view to putting the state's economy on a wartime basis. The same year, Gov. Whitemarsh B. Seabrook recommended the expulsion of all free blacks who owned no real estate or slave property.

Their continued residence among us, if the warfare between the North and South is to continue, will eventually generate evils difficult of eradication. Possessing in an unlimited degree the right of locomotion, they can in person bear intelligence on a day, from one section of a State to another, or through the post office mature their own plans of villainy, as well as execute orders emanating from foreign sources. There is indeed, too much reason to believe, that at this moment they are made to occupy the situation of spies in our camp.[27]

As tension mounted, the popular clamor against free blacks increased. Between 1856 and 1859 seventeen grand juries called to the attention of the legislature the dangers existing within the free colored population. No longer did petitioners advocate a trimming of freedom; without exception, they demanded the removal or enslavement of the state's free blacks. The exigencies of the sectional crisis convinced South Carolinians that "We should have but

[26] Stirling, *Letters from the Slave States*, pp. 299–300; William Chambers, *American Slavery and Colour* (London, 1857), pp. 205–6; Woodson, *Free Negro Heads of Families*, pp. xxv–xxx; John Hope Franklin, *From Slavery to Freedom*, p. 219.

[27] Anne King Gregorie, *History of Sumter County*, p. 161; Howell Meadows Henry, *Police Control of the Slave in South Carolina*, p. 186.

two classes, the Master and the slave, and no intermediate class can be other than immensely mischievous to our peculiar institution."[28]

In 1859 and 1860 two bills were debated in the legislature—the one to authorize free blacks to select their owners and to go into slavery, the other to provide for the temporary sale of "vicious and vagrant free persons of color."[29] The lag between popular demand and official policy had finally been bridged and the debate concluded. To the free black it seemed that the straits of freedom had led him to a dead-end. For him, no intervention was more timely than the explosion which in 1861 began to shatter the peculiar institution.

[28] Grand Jury Presentments, Kershaw District, Fall Term 1856, Fall Term 1857, Fall Term 1859; Greenville District, Spring Term 1859; Newberry District, Spring Term 1859; Chesterfield District, Spring Term 1859; Edgefield District, Fall Term 1859; Fairfield District, Spring Term 1858; Williamsburg District, Spring Term 1859; York District, Fall Term 1858, Extra Term 1858, Fall Term 1859; Sumter District, n.d.; Anderson District, October Term 1858, Fall Term 1859; Beaufort District, Fall Term 1859; Charleston District, October Term 1859.

[29] Reports of the Committee on the Colored Population, Dec. 17, 1859; Dec. 8, 1860, in Reports of Committees of the South Carolina Legislature.

CHAPTER IX

Escape from Freedom

THE DECADE OF THE 1850s THREATENED TO DEPRIVE THE free black of the precarious freedom he had previously enjoyed. He was presented now with the restricted alternatives of enslavement or exile. And exile in this period indicated that he must remove himself from the country altogether, unless he was wealthy enough to find a place on a packet leaving Charleston for a Northern port, for restrictions on free blacks in the neighboring states made travel northwards or westwards by land virtually impossible. His situation might well be summed up in a latter-day version of the American Colonization Society's theme: Liberia or Bust!

The pressures of this decade only enhanced the attractions of emigration. The free black's status in a slave society had always been insecure. The options now forced upon him had been taken voluntarily by many free blacks in previous decades. Inevitably contrasting the "free" society of the North with the slave system, free blacks had drifted to Northern cities in search of greater opportunity and a less ambiguous freedom. Some of them had emigrated beyond the United States—to Haiti, where the black man held his own, and to Canada, where immunity from the Fugitive Slave Law gave the black the security he lacked in the United States. There were also the virgin lands of Africa, the promise of a return to the homeland, brought to the black courtesy of the American Colonization Society.

The prospect of enslavement was, of course, less attractive. Admittedly, some favored house slaves enjoyed a security and protection that was denied the free black. They were clothed, fed and housed by their masters and sometimes they enjoyed an intimacy and a sense of belonging in the household. The future held little else for them beyond that dependence; their security could be consummated only by freedom, for close household ties did not insure them against the fluctuations of a plantation economy and the attending slave auction. The free black might have to fend for himself in a highly competitive market, but his labor was his own, and he had a freedom of movement that the most favored house slave never enjoyed. There is no evidence before the 1850s of the voluntary enslavement of free blacks.

Within South Carolina, the atmosphere was becoming increasingly hostile. Legislative restrictions were mild, by comparison with those in other slave states, but in his everyday life the free black had to contend with discrimination, exclusion from the professions and certain other occupations, and social customs which insisted that, whether slave or free, the black should manifest a subordination toward the white. If the free black was economically independent, he was also subject to social, religious and moral repression. It was natural that he should seek to escape from this straitjacket.

Escape was hedged about, however, by a multiplicity of conditions. Emigration to Liberia required capital for transportation and for the purchase of land, which would be his only insurance against destitution. While the American Colonization Society underwrote to a limited extent his survival in Liberia, the free black who migrated to Canada or Haiti was completely on his own and must be equipped also for the cultural transition attending emigration. The largest number of free black émigrés remained in the United States and went North, but the need for contacts, capital and, above all, a skill which would enable them to survive was greatest in these instances. Like the choice of enslavement, which the free black did not utilize until the end of the antebellum period, the option of exile was irrevocable, for the laws of South Carolina absolutely prohibited the return of free blacks who left the state for any reason whatever.

The American Colonization Society had been founded for the purpose of colonizing the free people of color of the United States. Its motives have been a subject of much controversy, an issue which is not within the purview of this study. However, the fact that the original impulse for colonization came from the slave state of Virginia suggests an attitude toward the free black that was not purely humanitarian. Neither Virginia nor any other slave state was disposed to protect its free colored population. Free blacks had always been considered a threat to slave property. Legislation in the Southern states throughout the antebellum period, and particularly during its last decade, reveals the underlying desire to be rid of the anomaly which challenged the foundation of the slave system and allegedly threatened the security of the white population. Liberia was no more an asylum for free blacks than it was an escape hatch for the custodians of slavery. Even Northern antislavery reformers found it an easy way out of the dilemma into which they had been forced by the moral issue of slavery and the practical issue of absorbing the black into white society. In 1840, twenty-four years after the founding of the American Colonization Society, William Jay very shrewdly summed up the free black's position in the movement:

The oppressor of the free negro dwells on his depravity and degradation; the friend of the free negro admits, and often aggravates the charges against him, but carefully abstains from all allusion to the true causes of that depravity, unless to excuse them as being inevitable. Both parties unite in depicting in glowing colors the effects of the oppression of the free negro in order to prove the *humanity* of banishing him from the country, while both refrain from all attempts to remove or lessen the oppression.[1]

The debate on colonization hardly touched the Southern black. It is significant that Northern blacks, exempt from the immediate pressures of slavery, presented an organized opposition to the society's ventures.[2] But the Southern black was aware only of the new world of opportunity opened up for him outside the confines of the peculiar institution. A free black of Charleston, urging his fellow denizens to migrate in 1832, predicted a black settlement of Africa paralleling the white colonization of North America. Looking into his own state, the would-be pioneer pointed to the success of the numerous Scotch-Irish, Swiss, German and French immigrants. "Many who arrive here very poor are soon made rich, and so it will be with us in Liberia," he anticipated. "Your reputation as a body of first-rate mechanics, is well known; distinguished

---

[1] William Jay, *Inquiry into the Character and Tendency of the American Colonization and American Anti-Slavery Societies*, p. 13.

[2] John Hope Franklin, *From Slavery to Freedom*, p. 236; Leon F. Litwack, *North of Slavery*, pp. 24–27, 235.

for your industry . . . you have with you carpenters, millers, wheel-wrights, ship-builders, engineers, cabinet-makers, shoe-makers, tailors and a host of others, all calculated at once to make you a great people."[3]

To the great majority of Southern blacks, slave and free, Liberia held the promise of freedom and relief from oppression. Although the African slave had undergone a steady process of Americanization, the prospect of a return to the homeland must have seemed the fulfillment of a dream. For the many who had completely absorbed the outlook of the predominant white society migration to Africa assumed a new perspective: the Americanized African took up the white man's burden and turned his steps toward his benighted brethren. One free black of Virginia wrote to the Colonization Society, "I wish to Go to Liberia So as I may teach Sinners the way of Salvation and also Educate my children and ingoy the Right of a man." He merely expressed a happy synthesis of the ideals he had imbibed from white society.[4] On a more organized level, in 1831 a group of wealthy, educated free blacks in Charleston decided to form an association for the promotion of emigration to Liberia. The chairman announced the objectives of the association at its first meeting: "The inhabitants [previous immigrants] invite us to come and possess it [Liberia] and to assist them to infuse into the natives notions of pure morality and to erect temples dedicated to the worship of Jehovah." At the same meeting members unanimously issued the clarion call to fellow free blacks: "Tarry thou not, but come over and dispel the darkness from your benighted land."[5]

[3] *African Repository and Colonial Journal,* VIII (October 1832), pp. 239–43.

[4] Carter G. Woodson, ed., *The Mind of the Negro as Reflected in Letters Written During the Crisis, 1800–1860,* pp. 93–94.

[5] *African Repository,* VIII (May 1832+), pp. 74–75.

The Colonization Society had made little headway in South Carolina thus far, but the local association of free blacks met with singular success in the first year of its being. One hundred and eighty blacks, slave and free, left for Liberia in 1832. This success was short-lived, however. In 1833, the ship *Jupiter*, which had transported the first group of emigrants, listed only two blacks from South Carolina on its second voyage, and it is likely that this sudden lull in emigration was influenced by unfavorable news of the pioneer émigrés. For the next nine years no blacks left South Carolina for Liberia. The total prohibition of manumission in 1841 and the restrictions it portended may have renewed the enthusiasm for emigration, for in 1842 forty-two blacks left for Liberia. The next two decades saw a steady emigration, 126 blacks migrating in the 1840s, and 110 in the 1850s. The exact proportion of free blacks to slaves is not known, but if the year 1849 may be regarded as average, the numbers were equal. Figures for the 1850s do not indicate that the heightening hostility to free blacks induced greater emigration to Liberia. In 1860, however, twenty-six free blacks, an unusually large number for any year after 1832, left South Carolina on the ship *Stevens*.[6]

Many of the free blacks who left the state for Liberia were men of some means who were able to finance the transportation of their families as well. All of the adult male free black emigrants who left in May 1849 were economically independent, among them a number of farmers, some tailors, carpenters, draymen, blacksmiths and butchers. Almost half could read or write or do both.[7] The émigrés represented neither the restless nor the under-

[6] Woodson, ed., *The Mind of the Negro*, pp. 81–83; *African Repository*, XXV (July 1849), pp. 220–21, XXXIII (May 1857), pp. 152–55; *Forty-Second Annual Report of the American Colonization Society*, pp. 53–56.

[7] *African Repository*, XXV (July 1849), pp. 220–21.

privileged among the free black population, as one writer has recently claimed.[8] Perhaps the most typical of the émigré group was the free black of Charleston who wrote to the Colonization Society, "i wants to go to Sinoe being i am related to Richard Murray i am in a situation and i have give notice that i am going i have a small piece of ground and have made arraingment even for to sell it." Liberia promised more to the free black than freedom from oppression; it represented, rather, the door to opportunity wherein he might not only better his material prospects but attain the self-respect denied him in South Carolina.[9] Members of the free black elite were sometimes inclined to give up the economic security they enjoyed in the state in the hope of finding social status or greater economic prosperity in Africa. As early as 1821, when colonization offered little security to any black, George Creighton, a wealthy free black barber of considerable reputation, sold his establishment and announced his willingness to emancipate his slaves if they would go to Liberia with him. Even a man of Jehu Jones' reputation abandoned his lucrative business in Charleston for the post of editor on a newspaper that the Colonization Society proposed to publish in Liberia.[10] Jones was perhaps the best-known free black in Charleston and enjoyed a status that was not usually accorded the city's free blacks, but his decision suggests that, even at its best, the social status of the free black in South Carolina remained ambiguous.

Not all of these men were successful. Jones' own fate was a sorry one. He never got beyond New York, where he was

---

[8] E. Horace Fitchett, "The Free Negro in Charleston, South Carolina," (Ph.D. diss., University of Chicago, 1950), p. 243.

[9] Woodson, ed., *Mind of the Negro*, pp. 94–95.

[10] Carter G. Woodson, *Free Negro Heads of Families*, p. xxxv; Document B, Documents Relating to the Vesey Uprising; Petition of Jehu Jones, a free person of color, 1840, in Petitions Relating to Slavery.

stranded by the Colonization Society, and, prohibited from returning to South Carolina, he was forced to sell all his property in the state and to live in virtual exile.[11] Little is known of those who did reach Liberia. The accounts published by the society were intended to encourage further settlement and rarely provide a description of actual conditions in the settlement. Settlers had to contend with an unfamiliar climate, disease, the immediate need to make a living and the general problem of making a cultural transition. But the steady migration after 1840 suggests that, risk and hardship notwithstanding, free blacks were eager to utilize an option which provided the barest hope of a freer life than that afforded them by the state of South Carolina.

The society met with a degree of competition from a rival group which proposed emigration to Central America as an alternative to the "back to Africa" movement. The venture achieved some popularity in the 1850s, and in 1854 an organization was formed with delegates from Canada, the Northern states and three of the slave states attending its first convention. It was hoped that the opportunity to remain in the New World would attract the blacks who were chary of uprooting themselves for the promise of a better life. Yet, despite the efforts of Francis Preston Blair in Congress and the enthusiasm of propagandists like Martin R. Delaney, the movement never seriously challenged the better-organized American Colonization Society. An initial settlement was established in Greytown, on the Mosquito reservation, in the 1850s, but the combined effects of climate, disease and a bombarding United States naval squadron took their toll. Lacking the influence of local agencies in South Carolina, the move-

[11] Petition of Jehu Jones, a free person of color, 1840, in Petitions Relating to Slavery.

ment never had any real appeal to free blacks in the state, even at the height of the sectional crisis.[12]

A more successful emigration to Canada was launched in 1829, and within two years the settlement of Wilberforce in Upper Canada constituted the nucleus of a rapidly expanding black colony.[13] There is no evidence of an organized emigration among the free blacks of South Carolina; on the other hand, a considerable number of individuals made their way to Canada, where they hoped to shake off the shackles of racial prejudice. Emigration was particularly attractive to free black partners in racially mixed marriages, who found that the tolerance of an earlier period was rapidly diminishing under the pressure of the sectional crisis. The daughter of Jane Wightman, a very wealthy free black of Charleston, married a Scot and moved with her family to a less-inhibited life in the city of Montreal.[14] The children of William Ellison, who had married a white, found it more feasible to emigrate, although Ellison himself had been well received in white society. Success was not always assured, however. One of the grandsons of Richard Holloway left his family's thriving carpentry establishment to make his fortune as a Canadian trader. Eventually compelled to declare insolvency in 1856, he had to fall back on the support of a solicitous grandmother in Charleston.[15]

While emigration to distant places like Canada, Liberia or Central America presented many financial problems to the average free black, emigration to the North was comparatively easier. Regular packets sailed from the port of

[12] Woodson, *Mind of the Negro*, pp. 494–504; Frank A. Rollin, *The Life and Public Services of Martin R. Delaney*, p. 80.

[13] *African Repository*, VIII (May 1832), pp. 225–27.

[14] Will of Jane Wightman, Record of Wills (Charleston County), Vol. 46, Book A, 1851–56, pp. 258–60; Will of Henry C. Gefkin, ibid., Vol. 47, Book B, 1851–56, p. 691.

[15] The Holloway Scrapbook.

Charleston to Philadelphia and New York, and many free
blacks availed themselves of this mode of transportation.[16]
Both cities had large black populations, and free blacks
who left South Carolina for the North would be more
easily absorbed into the local colored population than they
would be in Northern rural areas. Even so, the free black's
prospects for making a living in Northern cities were
hardly fair. In a Southern market accustomed to black
labor, free blacks who were willing to work for lower
wages held an advantage over white artisans and laborers.
In the North, competition was intensified by the vast numbers of white immigrants who flooded the labor market.
Despite the fact that most free blacks who left South
Carolina for the North were skilled artisans, they could
find little opportunity for work outside the demand for
unskilled labor. This was due, in part, to the strong resentment that white artisans bore toward their black com-
petitors. White workers frequently refused to accept blacks
as apprentices and resisted the efforts of their employers
to hire the black on equal terms. Even an outstanding
black like Frederick Douglass, who had been a skilled
caulker as a slave, could not find work in the New Bed-
ford shipyards because of the fear that white workers
would object. For three years he worked as a laborer, a
coachman and, later, as a waiter.[17] Coupled with the element of racial prejudice, so strong was the competition
in the North that a black leader in Boston complained in
1860 that it was ten times as difficult for a colored mechanic to find work in Boston as it was in Charleston.[18]

Even the better-equipped free black emigrant found
that the lure of opportunity in the North was highly de-

[16] Helen T. Catteral, ed., *Judicial Cases Concerning American Slavery
and the Negro*, II, pp. 345, 420–21.
[17] Litwack, *North of Slavery*, pp. 157–58.
[18] Ibid., p. 110.

ceptive. Allen Bland had received a good education in Charleston, through private tuition he received from a graduate of the College of Charleston. On the completion of his education, his father had sent him to Philadelphia "in the view of his having Superior Opportunities to improve his mind and be placed in a sphere of usefullness." But the younger Bland languished in Philadelphia with hope of neither education nor employment, and in 1848 the distraught father pleaded with the Colonization Society to take his son into its service and send him to Liberia.[19]

A second member of the Holloway family came to grief when, equipped with a considerable amount of cash and material possessions, he set out to make his fortune in New York. In 1829 he wrote to a friend that "business in this part is extremely dull at this season and so much so with me that I have not earned these two months $2." Although a skilled carpenter, he had not been able to make a living at his trade for three years. Unable to survive in New York, prohibited by law from reentering the state of South Carolina, and too ashamed to return to Charleston even if he could prevail on influential white patrons to obtain permission for his reentry, he decided eventually to join the free black group in New Orleans.[20]

The few free blacks who did survive the economic struggle in the North found few social rewards. Racial discrimination was as strong in the North, if more covert than in the South. Hostility was particularly strong toward the free blacks who migrated northward. In 1821, a committee of the Massachusetts legislature reported that immigrant Southern blacks were responsible for the increased

[19] Woodson, ed., *Mind of the Negro*, p. 74.
[20] Francis Huger to James ———, New York, Sept. 1, 1829, Holloway Scrapbook.

number of convicts and paupers, for indolence and dis-
orderliness in the towns and for the displacement of the
regular white employees in the state. The legislature was
urged to close the state to immigrant free blacks as the
Southern states of Virginia and South Carolina had done.
Reviewing the controversy, the South Carolinian biog-
rapher of Robert Hayne observed that "it is indisputable
that a higher and nobler type of colored man was being
developed in South Carolina than in Massachusetts." If
the findings of the Massachusetts legislature are carried to
their logical conclusion, however, it is evident that South
Carolina's free blacks became degenerate the moment they
touched Northern soil![21]

If emigration abroad entailed the difficulties of a cultural transition, migration to the North created equally
difficult problems of adjustment to Northern society. In
1839, a black South Carolinian bemoaned the fate of emigrant free blacks who were "digging out a miserable
existence in the northern cities." Having settled in Philadelphia, he found that the law in his adopted city "when
applied to colored people in opposition to white people is
not as good as in Charleston." The free black could not
rent a house in a square occupied by white people, he was
denied access to the museum and other public places and
the only advantage he enjoyed was that if his family was
ill he could send for a doctor at any time of night without
a pass. He concluded,

I am free to say, that not one of us who left Charleston with
high expectations to improve our condition . . . have but entirely failed in their expectations, in fact, so different is the
living at the north from that of the south . . . that Carolini-

21 *City Gazette* (Charleston) , July 27, 1821; Theodore D. Jervey, *Robert
Y. Hayne and His Times*, p. 117.

ans cannot live comfortably at the north, for this very plain reason. The manners, habits and pursuits of the people are so vastly different. . . . He does not find happiness in these cold regions, where prejudice against the colored complexion reigns triumphant, no matter what a man professes to be, he keeps far off from colored people. . . .[22]

Finding little redress outside South Carolina, the state's free blacks had one further option: voluntary enslavement. Between 1859 and 1863 a remarkable number of free blacks petitioned the legislature for permission to go into slavery. There is no evidence that the option had been utilized before this period and it is possible that fear of the impending sectional crisis drove the now suspect free black to seek the protection of a master before his security was further jeopardized. With the single exception of a free black boy, moreover, who laconically explained that he was "tired of freedom and wish to become a slave," the petitioners were all women, encumbered with families and having no means of support.[23] The legislature was more than willing to accommodate them; recent debates revealed that the state was beginning to believe that enslavement was the only viable option for free blacks.[24] The sectional crisis had begun to shake the institution of slavery to its very foundations; its ramifications—the police system, judicial procedures, religious organizations and, chiefly, the free black community—began to suc-

---

[22] Woodson, *Mind of the Negro*, pp. 10–13; *African Repository*, XV (March 1839), pp. 178–80.

[23] Petitions of William Jackson (free boy of color), 1861, Lucy Andrews, 1859, 1861, 1863, Elizabeth Bugg, 1860, Charles O. Lamotte on behalf of Lizzie Jones, 1859, Elizabeth Jane Berg, 1859, in Petitions Relating to Slavery.

[24] Petitions of Charles O. Lamotte on behalf of Lizzie Jones, 1859, Elizabeth Jane Berg, 1859, Daniel Freeman, 1860; Bill to authorize voluntary enslavement, 1859, in Petitions Relating to Slavery.

cumb to the upheaval well before the Civil War actually shattered the institution.

The precarious liberty that the free black had enjoyed crumbled under the impact of the Civil War. The exigencies of the war penetrated the group, as "secesh" and "union" factions clashed within over an issue that seemingly revolved on the Afro-American's freedom. But the ordeal yielded a larger and better-knit group of blacks than had existed previously in South Carolina. The liberty which had distinguished the free black group had also separated it from the larger mass of blacks. Beset by legislative restrictions, social discrimination and the inability to identify with their race, the free blacks of South Carolina had enjoyed a dubious freedom. That freedom was consummated when the mortgage of liberty was redeemed for the whole black race.

APPENDIXES

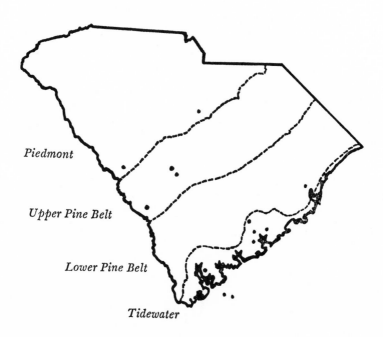

Piedmont

Upper Pine Belt

Lower Pine Belt

Tidewater

SOUTH CAROLINA FREE NEGRO POPULATION *1790*
Scale • = 200

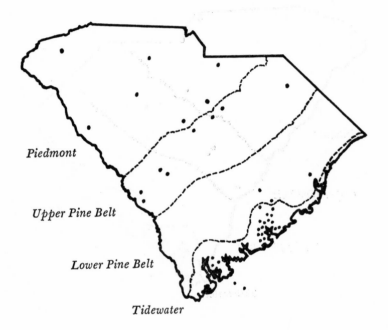

Piedmont

Upper Pine Belt

Lower Pine Belt

Tidewater

SOUTH CAROLINA FREE NEGRO POPULATION *1830*
Scale • = 200

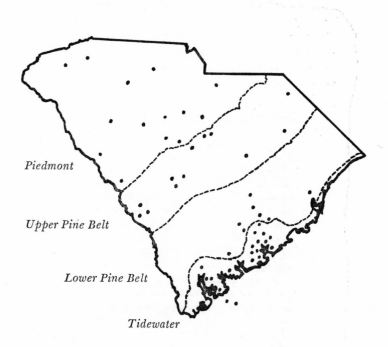

Piedmont

Upper Pine Belt

Lower Pine Belt

Tidewater

SOUTH CAROLINA FREE NEGRO POPULATION *1860*
Scale • = 200

APPENDIX B

Certificate of Freedom
(Reproduced with the kind permission of
Mrs. Naomi Johnston Brown.)

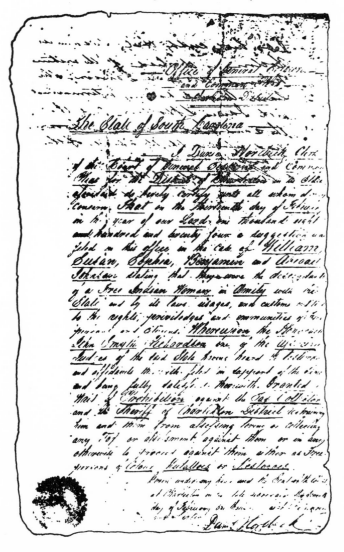

Register of Transient Sick and City Poor, Charleston Alms House*

Date of Admission	Name	By Whose Order	Occu-pation	Date of Discharge
1807, Feb. 2	William Seymour	Mr. Magwood	——	——
1809, Aug. 3	Will Taggert	Mr. Price	——	Aug. 24, 1809
1811, June 11	Clara	Mr. Johnson	——	Dec. 10, 1811
1811, June 10	Samuel Johnson	Mr. Johnson	——	June 20, 1811
1812, Sept. 2	Salley Watts	City Marshall	——	——
1812, Nov. 12	Lyon (a Moor)	Mr. Cleary	——	——
1813, Jan. 25	Captain Brown (an Indian)	Mr. Magwood	——	Jan. 26, 1813
1813, June 4	Adam Nowel (a black)	City Marshall	——	Sept. 10, 1813
1814, June 19	Zealy	——do—— (from St. Domingo)	——	Jan. 16, 1815
1815, Oct. 17	Isaac Lowry	——	——	Nov. 7, 1815
1819, April 7	Nelly	——	——	Nov. 3, 1819
1819, July 15	Ben Baker	——	——	July 17, 1819
1820, Oct. 9	Carlos	——	——	Oct. 14, 1820
1820, Oct. 28	Carlos	——	——	Oct. 20, 1820
1820, Nov. 18	Carlos	——	——	Dec. 6, 1820
1820, Nov. 21	Beck	——	——	Sept. 2, 1821

* South Carolina Historical Society

The Certificate of Freedom of Jacob and Elizabeth Bell

City of Charleston, Affidavit of Archibald Brown Lord before Benjamin Elfe certifying the freedom of Jacob Bell and family, 19 November 1831. Legislative Papers. Reproduced by permission of the South Carolina Archives Department, Columbia, S.C.

Sale of a Free Black for Tax Default

State of South-Carolina,

By *(signature)*

BY HENRY L. PINCKNEY, ESQUIRE,

COLLECTOR OF THE GENERAL TAX FOR THE PARISHES OF ST. PHILIP AND ST. MICHAEL.

To *(blank)*, Esq., Sheriff of Charleston District, or his Lawful Deputy.

WHEREAS, a Tax of Two dollars has been laid, by an Act of 18__, upon all Free Negroes, Mulattoes and Mustizoes, between the ages of 15 and 50, for defraying the charges of the State, which Capitation Tax *(name)* a person of color, has neglected to pay. *THESE are therefore*, in the name of the State, strictly to charge and command you to take into your custody the body of the said *John Daingerfield* and sell *his* Services, for a term not exceeding One Year, and not for a longer time than shall be necessary to pay the said Capitation Tax, together with the lawful costs and charges thereon. And for your so doing this shall be your sufficient *WARRANT*.

Given under my Hand and Seal, at the General Tax Office, Charleston,
the __ day of __ 1852.

(signature)

General Tax, do.	$4,00	
Neck Capit. do.		
Road do.	.16	
Poor do.		
Cross-Road. do.	.12	
Pub. Build. do.		
Free School do.		
	4.28	
Execution,	.55	

[L.S.]

Warrant of Olney Harleston to Sheriff of Charleston District for sale of John Daingerfield for tax default, 7 June 1852. Legislative Papers. Reproduced by permission of South Carolina Archives Department, Columbia, S.C.

BIBLIOGRAPHY

Manuscripts

Charleston. Certificate of freedom of William, Susan, Sophia, Benjamin and Abigail Johnson, 1824. In possession of Mrs. Naomi Johnston Brown.

Charleston. Diary of Richmond Kinloch. In possession of Mrs. Julia De Costa.

Charleston. Holloway Scrapbook. In possession of Mrs. Mae Holloway Purcell.

Charleston. South Carolina Historical Society. James Louis Pettigru papers.

Charleston. South Carolina Historical Society. Letters of "Rusticus," 1794.

Charleston. South Carolina Historical Society. Records of the Poor House, Charleston County, 1847–60.

Charleston. South Carolina Historical Society. Records Relating to the Brown Fellowship Society.

Charleston. Charleston County Courthouse. Register of Mesne Conveyance, 1790–1860.

Charleston. South Carolina Historical Society. Register of the Transient Sick and Poor of the Charleston Alms House, 1807–50.

Columbia. South Carolina Archives Department. British Public Record Office Transcripts, Vol. 35.

Columbia, S.C. South Carolina Archives Department. Confederate Muster Rolls.

Columbia, S.C. South Carolina Archives Department. Corre-

spondence of the Governor of South Carolina with the
French Assembly in St. Domingo, 1791–93.

Columbia, S.C. South Carolina Archives Department. Court of
Appeals, Decrees in Equity Cases, 1832–35.

Columbia, S.C. South Carolina Archives Department. Documents Relating to the Denmark Vesey Uprising, 1822.

Columbia, S.C. South Carolina Archives Department. Documents Relating to the Free Moors of South Carolina.

Columbia, S.C. South Carolina Archives Department. Grand
Jury Presentments, 1790–1865.

Columbia, S.C. South Carolina Archives Department. Journals
of the Senate and House of Representatives of South Carolina, 1790–1865.

Columbia, S.C. South Carolina Archives Department. Messages of the Governors of South Carolina to the State Legislature, 1790–1865.

Columbia, S.C. South Carolina Archives Department. Miscellaneous Records of Wills, Deeds, Inventories, etc.

Columbia, S.C. South Carolina Archives Department. Miscellaneous Tax Returns.

Columbia, S.C. University of South Carolina. The South Caroliniana Library. Noisette papers.

Columbia, S.C. South Carolina Archives Department. Petitions
Relating to Slavery, 1790–1865.

Columbia, S.C. South Carolina Archives Department. Records
of St. Philip's Episcopal Church, 1713–1940.

Columbia, S.C. South Carolina Archives Department. Register
of the Episcopal Church of St. George Winyah, 1813–1916.

Columbia, S.C. South Carolina Archives Department. Reports
of the Committees of the South Carolina Legislature, 1790–
1865.

Columbia, S.C. South Carolina Archives Department. Statutes
at Large.

Columbia, S.C. South Carolina Archives Department. The
Free Negro Book: Records of the Comptroller-General of
the State of South Carolina, 1816, 1819, 1823, 1824, 1833,
1851.

Columbia, S.C. South Carolina Archives Department. Unpublished Agriculture Schedules of the Seventh Census.

Columbia, S.C. South Carolina Archives Department. Unpublished Industry Schedules of the Seventh Census.

Washington, D.C. Library of Congress. Revolutionary War Pensions.

Public Documents

A Collection of Ordinances of the City Council of Charleston 1818–1823. Charleston, 1823.

Cauthen, Charles E., ed. *The State Records of South Carolina, Journals of the South Carolina Executive Councils of 1861 and 1862*. Columbia, S.C., 1956.

Dawson, J. L., and H. W. De Saussure, ed. *Census of the City of Charleston, South Carolina for 1848*. Charleston, 1849.

De Bow, J. D. B., ed. *Compendium of the Seventh Census of the United States*. Washington, D.C., 1854.

Digest of the Ordinances of the City Council of Charleston. Charleston, 1818.

Digest of the Ordinances of the City Council of Charleston From the years 1783 to October 1844. To Which are Annexed the Acts of the Legislature Which Relate Exclusively to the City of Charleston. Charleston, 1844.

Eighth Federal Census of the United States. Washington, D.C., 1861.

Fifth Federal Census of the United States. Washington, D.C., 1831.

First Federal Census of the United States. Washington, D.C., 1791.

Fourth Federal Census of the United States. Washington, D.C., 1821.

Hamilton, James, Jr. *An Account of the Late Intended Insurrection Among A Portion of the Blacks of this City. Published by the Authority of the Corporation of Charleston*. 2d ed. Charleston, 1822.

Kennedy, Lionel H., and Parker, Thomas. *An Official Report of the Trials of Sundry Negroes, Charged With an Attempt to Raise an Insurrection in the State of South Carolina Preceded by an Introduction and Narrative and in an Appendix a Report of the Trials of Four White Persons on Indictments For Attempting to Excite the Slaves to Insurrection. Prepared and Published at the Request of the Court by Lionel H. Kennedy and Thomas Parker.* Charleston, 1822.

McCord, David J., and Cooper, Thomas, eds. *The Statutes At Large of South Carolina; edited, Under Authority of the Legislature.* 10 vols. Columbia, S.C., 1836–1840.

Official Opinions of the Attorneys General of the United States. 40 vols. Washington, D.C., 1791–1948.

O'Neall, John Belton, ed. *The Negro Law of South Carolina, Collected and Digested by John Belton O'Neall, One of the Judges of the Courts of Law and Errors of the Said State, Under a Resolution of the State Agricultural Society of South Carolina.* Columbia, S.C., 1848.

Ordinances of the City of Charleston From the 14th September 1854 to the 1st. December, 1859. And the Acts of the General Assembly Relating to the City Council of Charleston and the City of Charleston during the same period. Compiled by John R. Horsey by Direction of the City Council. Charleston, 1859.

Records of Wills—Charleston County, Vols. I, LI; Richland County, Vols. I–III, in manuscripts of the South Carolina Archives Department.

Second Federal Census of the United States. Washington, D.C., 1801.

Seventh Federal Census of the United States. Washington, D.C., 1851.

Sixth Federal Census of the United States. Washington, D.C., 1841.

The Militia and Patrol Laws of South Carolina December 1844 Published by Order of the General Assembly. Columbia, S.C., 1845.

Third Federal Census of the United States. Washington, D.C. 1811.

Contemporary Sources

NEWSPAPERS

African Repository and Colonial Journal (Washington, D.C.), 1816–65.

Charleston Courier, 1803–18.

Charleston Mercury, 1825–62.

City Gazette and Daily Advertiser (Charleston), 1789–1832.

Edgefield (S.C.) *Advertiser*, 1836–65.

Marion (S.C.) *Star*, 1861.

Massachusetts Spy or Worcester Gazette, December 1797.

National Intelligencer (Washington, D.C.), 1820–32.

Niles' Weekly Register (Baltimore, Md.), 1819–40.

South Carolina State Gazette and Columbia Advertiser (Columbia, S.C.), 1824, 1825, 1829.

South Carolinian (Columbia, S.C.), 1838.

Southern Patriot (Greenville, S.C.), 1819–40.

The State. (Columbia, S.C.), Mar. 18, 1928.

BOOKS AND PAMPHLETS

A South Carolinian [Frederick Dalcho?]. *Practical Considerations Founded on the Scriptures Relative to the Slave Population of South Carolina. Respectfully Dedicated to "The South Carolina Association."* Charleston, 1823.

Achates [Thomas Pinckney?]. *Reflections Occasioned by the Late Disturbances in Charleston, by Achates.* Charleston, 1822.

Adams, F. C. *Manuel Pereira or The Sovereign Rule of South Carolina, With Views of Southern Laws, Life and Hospitality.* Washington, D.C., 1853.

Adger, John B. *My Life and Times, 1810–1899.* Richmond, 1899.

Cardozo, J. N. *Reminiscences of Charleston.* Charleston, 1866.

De Bow, J. D. B. *De Bow's Review; Agricultural, Commercial, Industrial Progress and Resources.* 42 vols. New Orleans. 1849–80.

Delaney, Martin R. *The Condition, Elevation, Emigration and Destiny of the Colored People of the United States.* Philadelphia, 1852.

Fitzhugh, George. *Sociology for the South, or the Failure of Free Society.* Richmond, 1854.

———. *What Shall be Done with the Free Negroes.* Fredericksburg, Va., 1851.

Fraser, Charles. *Reminiscences of Charleston.* Charleston, 1854.

Furman, Richard. *Exposition of the Views of the Baptists Relative to the Colored Population of the United States in a Communication to the Governor of South Carolina.* Charleston, 1823.

Grimke, Archibald H. *Right on the Scaffold, or the Martyrs of 1822.* Washington, D.C., 1901.

[Hamilton, T.] *"A Colored American." The Late Contemplated Insurrection in Charleston, South Carolina, with the Execution of Thirty-Six of the Patriots, etc.* New York, 1850.

Holland, E. C. *A Refutation of the Calumnies Circulated Against the Southern and Western States Respecting the Institution of Slavery, etc.* Charleston, 1822.

Hundley, Daniel R. *Social Relations in Our Southern States.* New York, 1860.

Jay, William. *Inquiry into the Character and Tendency of the American Colonization and American Anti-Slavery Societies.* New York, 1840.

Jones, Charles Colcock. *The Religious Instruction of the Negroes.* Savannah, 1842.

———. *Suggestions on the Religious Instruction of the Negroes in the Southern States.* Philadelphia, 1847.

Lossing, Benjamin J. *The Pictorial Fieldbook of the Revolution.* 2 vols. New York, 1860.

Mood, F. A. *Methodism in Charleston.* Nashville, 1856.

Payne, Daniel A. *Recollections of Seventy Years.* Nashville, 1888.

——— [?]. *The History of the African Methodist Episcopal Church.* Nashville, 1891.

Poyas, Elizabeth Ann. *The Olden Time of Carolina, by the*

Octogenarian Lady of Charleston, South Carolina. Charleston, 1855.

Smith, William L. *Life at the South; or "Uncle Tom's Cabin" as it is.* Buffalo, N.Y., 1852.

Thornwell, Rev. Dr. [James Henley]. *A Review of Rev. J. G. Adger's Sermon on the Religious Instruction of the Colored Population.* Charleston, 1847.

Townsend, John. *The Doom of Slavery in the Union.* Charleston, 1860.

Trapier, Paul. *The Religious Instruction of the Black Population. The Gospel to be Given to Our Servants. A Sermon Preached in Several Protestant Episcopal Churches in Charleston on Sundays in July, 1847 by Rev. Paul Trapier in Charleston, etc.* Charleston, 1847.

Turnbull, Robert James. *The Crisis: or, Essays on the Usurpation of the Federal Government. By Brutus.* Charleston, 1827.

————, and A. E. Miller. *Caroliniensis.* Charleston, n.d.

Victor, Orville J. *A History of American Conspiracies: A Record of Treason, Insurrection, Rebellion etc. in the United States from 1760 to 1860.* New York, 1863.

Wilson, William Hasell. *Reminiscences of William Hasell Wilson, 1811–1902.* Edited by Elizabeth B. Pharo. Philadelphia, 1937.

Forty-Second Annual Report of the American Colonization Society, with the Proceedings of the Board of Directors and of the Society. Washington, D.C., 1859.

Proceedings of the Meeting in Charleston, South Carolina, May 13–15, 1845, on the Religious Instruction of the Negroes together with the Report of the Committee and the Address to the Public. Charleston, 1845.

The Directory and Stranger's Guide, for the City of Charleston, For the Year 1794, To which is added An Almanac; the Tariff Duties on all Goods Imported into the United States; Rates of Wharfage, Weighing, and Storage, Cartage and Drayage etc. etc. Charleston, 1794.

The Directory and Stranger's Guide for the City of Charleston,

Also a Directory for Charleston Neck, Between Boundary Street and the Lines, For the Year 1819. To which is added An Almanac; the Tariff Duties on all Goods Imported into the United States; Rates of Wharfage, Weighing, and Storage, Cartage and Drayage etc. etc. Charleston, 1819.

Directory, or Guide to the Residences and Places of Business of the Inhabitants of the City of Charleston and its Environs: Prefaced with a Description of Our Various Public Buildings and other Local information. Taken down for the Year of Our Lord 1829. Charleston, 1829.

Directory and Stranger's Guide for the City of Charleston and Its Vicinity. Compiled by Morris Goldsmith. Charleston, 1831.

Rules and Regulations of the Brown Fellowship Society established at Charleston, South Carolina, 1st November, 1790. Charleston, 1844.

Rules and Regulations of the Friendly Moralist Society. Charleston, 1848.

Constitution and By-Laws of the Friendly Union Society of Charleston, South Carolina. Charleston, 1889.

The By-Laws or Constitutional Form of Government of The Episcopal Church of St. Philip. Charleston, 1805.

Travel Accounts

Abbott, John S. *South and North; or Impressions Received During a Trip to Cuba and the South.* New York, 1860.

Abdy, Edward S. *Journal of a Residence and Tour in the United States of North America from April 1833 to October 1834.* London, 1835.

Arese, Francisco. *A Trip to the Prairies in the Interior of North America.* New York, 1834.

Ashworth, Henry. *A Tour in the United States, Cuba and Canada.* London, 1861.

Baxter, William E. *America and the Americans.* London, 1855.

Benwell, J. *An Englishman's Travels in America, His Observations of Life and Manners in the Free and Slave States.* London, 1853.

Bernhard, Karl, Duke of Saxe-Weimar-Eisenach. *Travels*

Through North America during the Years 1825 and 1826.
2 vols. Philadelphia, 1828.

Bremer, Frederika. *America of the Fifties: Letters by Frederika Bremer.* Edited by Adolph B. Benson. New York, 1924.

Chambers, William. *Things as they Are in America.* London, 1854.

———. *American Slavery and Colour.* London, 1857.

Davies, Ebenezer. *American Scenes and Christian Slavery.* London, 1849.

Fairpoint, Alfred. *Uncle Sam and His Country.* London, 1857.

Francois, Alexander du Frederic, Duke de La Rouchefoucault-Liancourt. *Travels Through the United States of America, the Country of the Iroquois, and Upper Canada in the Years 1795, 1796, and 1797.* London, 1799.

Grund, Francis. *The Americans in their Moral, Social and Political Relations.* London, 1837.

Hall, Basil. *Travels in North America, in the Years 1827 and 1828.* 3 vols. Edinburgh, 1829.

Hamilton, Thomas. *Men and Manners in America.* Philadelphia, 1833.

Lewis, George. *Impressions of America and American Churches.* Edinburgh, 1845.

Lipscomb, A. A. *North and South: Impressions of a Northern Society Upon a Southerner.* Mobile, Ala., 1853.

Lyell, Charles. *A Second Visit to the United States of North America.* 2 vols. London, 1855.

Mackay, Charles. *Life and Liberty in America.* London, 1859.

Mackie, John Milton. *From Cape Cod to Dixie and the Tropics.* New York, 1864.

Marryat, Frederick. *A Diary in America with Remarks on its Institutions.* London, 1839.

Mitchell, David W. *Ten Years Residence in the United States.* London, 1862.

Murray, Henry A. *Lands of the Slave and the Free.* London, 1855.

Olmsted, Frederick Law. *Journey in the Seaboard Slave States with Remarks on Their Economy.* New York, 1859.

———. *The Cotton Kingdom, a Traveller's Observations on*

Cotton and Slavery in the American Slave States. 2 vols.
London, 1861.

———. *A Journey in the Back Country.* New York, 1863.

Parsons, C. G. *Inside View of Slavery; or a Tour Among the
Planters.* Boston, 1855.

Pierson, George Wilson, ed. *Tocqueville and Beaumont in
America.* New York, 1938.

Pulszky, Francis, and Pulszky, Theresa. *White, Red and Black:
Sketches of American Society.* New York, 1853.

Saint-Amand, Mary Scott. *A Balcony in Charleston.* Richmond, 1841.

Stirling, James. *Letters from the Slave States.* London, 1857.

Tasistro, Louis Fitzgerald. *Random Shots and Southern
Breezes, Containing Critical Remarks on the Southern States
and Southern Institutions, with Some Serious Observations
on Men and Manners.* 2 vols. New York, 1842.

Secondary Sources

BOOKS

Aptheker, Herbert. *Negro Slave Revolts in the United States,
1526–1860.* New York, 1939.

———. *The Negro in the Civil War.* New York, 1938.

Boykin, James H. *The Negro in North Carolina Prior to 1861,
an Historical Monograph.* New York, 1958.

Brawley, Benjamin C. *Negro Builders and Heroes.* Chapel
Hill, 1937.

Catteral, Helen T., ed. *Judicial Cases Concerning American
Slavery and the Negro.* 5 vols. Washington, D.C., 1926–37.

Church Annual of the Plymouth Congregational Church.
Charleston, 1925.

Collons, Winfield H. *Slavery and the Race Problem in the
South.* New York, 1904.

Drake, Thomas E. *Quakers and Slavery in America.* New
Haven, 1950.

DuBois, W. E. B. *The Souls of Black Folk.* Chicago, 1903.

Eaton, Clement. *The Mind of the Old South.* Baton Rouge,
1964.

Edwards, Maldwyn. *After Wesley: A Study of the Social and Political Influence of Methodism in the Middle Period (1791–1840)*. London, 1935.

Elkins, Stanley M. *Slavery; A Problem in American Institutional and Intellectual Life*. Chicago, 1959.

Fairly, John S. *The Negro in His Relations to the Church*. Charleston, 1889.

Fitchett, E. Horace. "The Free Negro in Charleston, South Carolina." Ph.D. diss., University of Chicago, 1950.

Fleming, William H. *Slavery and the Race Problem in the South*. Athens, Ga., 1906.

Franklin, John Hope. *From Slavery to Freedom, a History of American Negroes*. New York, 1950.

———. *The Free Negro in North Carolina, 1790–1860*. Chapel Hill, 1943.

Frazier, E. Franklin. *The Free Negro Family; a Study of Family Origins before the Civil War*. Nashville, 1932.

Gregorie, Anne King. *History of Sumter County*. Sumter, S.C., 1954.

Henry, Howell Meadows. *The Police Control of the Slave in South Carolina*. Emory, Va., 1914.

Hurd, John C. *Law of Freedom and Bondage in the United States*. 2 vols. New York, 1858–1862.

Jackson, Luther P. *Free Negro Labor and Property Holding in Virginia, 1830–1860*. New York, 1942.

Jenkins, W. S. *Pro-Slavery Thought in the Old South*. Chapel Hill, 1935.

Jervey, Theodore D. *Robert Y. Hayne and His Times*. New York, 1909.

———. *The Slave Trade, Slavery and Color*. Columbia, S.C., 1925.

Johnson, Franklin. *The Development of State Legislation Concerning the Free Negro*. New York, 1918.

Johnston, James H. *Miscegenation in the Ante-bellum South*. Chicago, 1939.

Jones, Frank D., and Mills, W. H., eds. *History of the Presbyterian Church in South Carolina Since 1850*. Columbia, S.C., 1926.

Klingberg, Frank J. *An Appraisal of the Negro in Colonial South Carolina; a Study in Americanization.* Washington, D.C., 1941.

Litwack, Leon F. *North of Slavery; the Negro in the Free States, 1790–1860.* Chicago, 1961.

Lofton, John. *Insurrection in South Carolina: the Turbulent World of Denmark Vesey.* Yellow Springs, Ohio, 1964.

McCrady, Edward G. *An Historic Church; the Westminster Abbey of South Carolina: A Sketch of St. Philip's Church.* Charleston, 1901.

Mannheim, Karl. *Ideology and Utopia: An Introduction to the Sociology of Knowledge.* Trans. from the German by Louis Wirth and Edward Shils. New York, 1936.

Mathews, Donald G. *Slavery and Methodism; a Chapter in American Morality, 1780–1845.* Princeton, 1965.

Meriwether, Robert L. *The Expansion of South Carolina, 1729–1765.* Kingsport, Tenn., 1940.

Merton, Robert K. *Social Theory and Social Structure.* London, 1957.

Morgan, Donald G. *Justice William Johnson; The First Dissenter: The Career and Constitutional Philosophy of a Jeffersonian Judge.* Columbia, S.C., 1954, 1971.

Nell, William C. *Colored Patriots of the American Revolution, with Sketches of Several Distinguished Colored Persons.* Boston, 1955.

Piettre, Andre. *Les trois âges de l'économie; essai sur les relations de l'économie et la civilisation de l'antiquité classique à nos jours; économie subordonée, économie independante, économie dirigée.* Paris, 1955.

Pike, James S. *The Prostrate State: South Carolina Under Negro Government.* New York, 1874.

Rainsford, Marcus. *An Historical Account of the Black Empire of Haiti, Comprehending a View of the Principal Transaction in the Revolution of Saint Domingo.* London, 1805.

Ravenal, Mrs. St. Julien. *Charleston, the Place and the People.* New York, 1906.

Reuter, Edward B. *Race Mixture; Studies in Intermarriage and Miscegenation.* New York, 1931.

Rollin, Frank A. *The Life and Public Services of Martin R. Delaney, Sub-Assistant Commissioner, Bureau Relief of Refugees, Freedom, and of Abandoned Lands, and Late Major 104th U.S. Colored Troops.* 2d ed. Boston, 1883.

Rose, Willie Lee. *Rehearsal for Reconstruction; the Port Royal Experiment.* Indianapolis, 1964.

Rousseve, Charles Barthelemy. *The Negro in Louisiana: Aspects of His History and His Literature.* New Orleans, 1937.

Russell, John. *The Free Negro in Virginia, 1619–1865.* Baltimore, 1913.

Shibutani, Tamotsu. "Reference Groups and Social Control." In Arnold M. Rose, ed., *Human Behavior and Social Processes.* Boston, 1962. Pp. 128–44.

Simmons, William J. *Men of Mark: Eminent, Progressive and Rising.* Cleveland, 1887.

Smith, D. E. Huger, and Salley, A. S., Jr., eds. *Register of St. Philip's Parish, 1754–1810.* Charleston, 1927, 1971.

Smith, Septima Chappell. "The Development and History of Some Negro Churches in South Carolina." M.A. thesis, University of South Carolina, 1942.

Souvenir Program of the One-Hundredth Anniversary of the Founding of the A.M.E. Church in the South held at Emmanuel A.M.E. Church. Charleston, 1963.

Some Historical Facts about St. Mark's Episcopal Church, Charleston, South Carolina. Charleston, 1965.

Stavisky, Leonard P. "The Negro Artisan in the South Atlantic States, 1800–1860; a Study of Status and Opportunity with Special Reference to Charleston." Ph.D. diss., Columbia University, 1958.

Stonequist, Everett V. *The Marginal Man.* New York, 1937.

Stroud, George M. *A Sketch of the Laws Relating to Slavery in the Several States of the United States.* 2d ed. Philadelphia, 1856.

Sumter, T. S. *Stateburg and Its People.* Sumter, S.C., 1949.

Sweat, Edward Forrest. "The Free Negro in Ante-bellum Georgia." Ph.D. diss., Indiana University, 1957.

Tannenbaum, Frank. *Slave and Citizen: the Negro in the Americas.* New York, 1946.

Taylor, Rosser Howard. *The Free Negro in North Carolina.* Chapel Hill, 1920.

———. *Ante-bellum South Carolina: A Social and Cultural History.* Chapel Hill, 1942.

Tindall, George B. *South Carolina Negroes, 1877–1900.* Columbia, S.C., 1952, 1970.

Wade, Richard C. *Slavery in the Cities; the South, 1820–1860.* New York, 1964.

Wearmouth, Robert F. *Methodism and the Working Class Movements of England, 1800–1850.* London, 1937.

———. *Methodism and the Common People of the Eighteenth Century.* London, 1945.

Wesley, Charles H. *Richard Allen, Apostle of Freedom.* Washington, D.C., 1935.

Wightman, William M. *The Life of William Capers.* Nashville, 1858.

Williamson, Joel. *After Slavery: The Negro in South Carolina during Reconstruction, 1861–1877.* Chapel Hill, 1965.

Wright, James M. *The Free Negro in Maryland, 1643–1860.* New York, 1921.

Wright, Richard R. *The Encyclopaedia of the African Methodist Episcopal Church.* Philadelphia, 1947.

Woodson, Carter G. *Free Negro Heads of Families in the United States in 1830.* Washington, D.C., 1925.

———. *Free Negro Owners of Slaves in the United States in 1830.* Washington, D.C., 1925.

———. *The Education of the Negro Prior to 1861; a History of the Education of the Colored People of the United States from the Beginning of Slavery to the Civil War.* New York, 1915.

———, ed. *The Mind of the Negro as Reflected in Letters Written During the Crisis, 1800–1860.* Washington, D.C., 1926.

——. *The Negro in Our History.* Washington, D.C., 1922.

Woodward, C. Vann. *The Strange Career of Jim Crow.* New York, 1957.

PERIODICALS

Anderson, J. P. "Public Education in Ante-Bellum South Carolina." *South Carolina Historical Association Proceeding* (1933), pp. 3–11.

Aptheker, Herbert. "South Carolina Poll Tax, 1737–1895." *Journal of Negro History,* XXXI (1946), pp. 131–39.

——. "South Carolina Negro Conventions 1865." *Journal of Negro History,* XXXI (1946), pp. 91–97.

——. "Maroons Within the Present Limits of the United States." *Journal of Negro History,* XXIV (April, 1939), pp. 167–83.

Berry, Brewton. "The Mestizos, South Carolina." *American Journal of Sociology,* LI (July 1945), pp. 34–41.

Birnie, C. W. "Education of the Negro in Charleston, South Carolina, Prior to the Civil War." *Journal of Negro History,* XII (January 1927), pp. 13–21.

Browning, James B. "The Beginnings of Insurance Enterprise among Negroes." *Journal of Negro History,* XXII, No. 4 (October 1937), pp. 417–32.

——. "The Free Negro in Ante Bellum North Carolina." *North Carolina Historical Review,* XV (1938), pp. 23–33.

——. "The North Carolina Black Code." *Journal of Negro History,* XV (1930), pp. 261–73.

Clarke, James Freeman. "Condition of the Free Colored People of the United States." *The Christian Examiner,* LXVL, 5th Ser., IV (1859), pp. 246–65.

Craven, Avery. "Poor Whites and Negroes in the Ante-Bellum South." *Journal of Negro History,* XV (1930), pp. 14–25.

Current, Richard N. "John C. Calhoun, Philosopher of Reaction." *Antioch Review,* III (Summer 1943), pp. 223–34.

Fitchett, E. Horace. "Traditions of the Free Negroes in Charleston, South Carolina." *Journal of Negro History,* XXV (April 1940), pp. 140–52.

Fitchett, E. Horace. "The Origin and Growth of the Free Negro Population of Charleston, South Carolina." *Journal of Negro History*, XXVI, No. 4 (October 1941), pp. 421–37.

Foster, Charles I. "The Colonization of Free Negroes in Liberia, 1816–1835." *Journal of Negro History*, XXXVIII (January 1953), pp. 41–66.

Hamer, Philip M. "Great Britain, the United States and the Negro Seamen Acts." *Journal of Southern History*, I (1916), pp. 3–28.

Hesseltine, William B. "Some New Aspects of the Pro-Slavery Argument." *Journal of Negro History*, XXI (January 1936), pp. 1–14.

Higginson, Thomas Wentworth. "Denmark Vesey." *Atlantic Monthly*, VII (1861), pp. 728–44.

Jackson, Luther P. "The Educational Efforts of the Freedmen's Bureau and Freedmen's Aid Societies in South Carolina, 1862–1870." *Journal of Negro History*, VIII (1923), pp. 1–40.

————. "The Religious Instruction of Negroes, 1830 to 1860, with Special Reference to South Carolina." *Journal of Negro History*, XV (January 1930), pp. 72–114.

————. "The Virginia Free Negro Farmer and Property Owner, 1830–1860." *Journal of Negro History*, XXIV (1939), pp. 390–439.

Litwack, Leon F. "The Federal Government and the Free Negro." *Journal of Negro History*, XLIII (1958), pp. 261–78.

Logan, Rayford W. "The Negro in the Quasi-War, 1798–1800." *Negro History Bulletin*, XIV (1951), pp. 128–31.

McKissick, J. R. "Some Observations of Travelers on South Carolina." *South Carolina Historical Association Proceedings* (1932), pp. 44–51.

Mehlinger, Louis R. "Attitudes of Free Negroes Toward Colonization." *Journal of Negro History*, I (1916), pp. 276–301.

Nelson, Alice Dunbar. "People of Color in Louisiana." *Journal of Negro History,* I (October 1916), pp. 361–76; II (1917), pp. 51–78.

Park, Robert E. "Human Migration and the Marginal Man." *American Journal of Sociology,* XXXIII, No. 6 (May 1928), pp. 881–93.

Phillips, Ulrich B. "The Slave Labor Problem in the Charleston District." *Political Science Quarterly,* XXII, No. 3 (September 1907), pp. 416–39.

Prior, Granville T. "Charleston Pastimes and Culture in the Nullification Decade, 1822–1832." *South Carolina Historical Association Proceedings* (1940), pp. 36–44.

Russell, John H. "Colored Freemen as Slave Owners in Virginia." *Journal of Negro History,* I (July 1916), pp. 233–42.

Sherwood, Henry N. "Early Negro Deportation Projects." *Mississippi Valley Historical Review,* II (1916), pp. 484–508.

Stonequist, Everett V. "The Problem of the Marginal Man." *American Journal of Sociology,* XLI, No. 1 (July 1935), pp. 1–12.

Sydnor, Charles. "The Free Negro in Mississippi Before the Civil War." *American Historical Review,* XXXII (July 1927), pp. 769–88.

Taylor, A. A. "Negro Congressmen a Generation After." *Journal of Negro History,* VII (1922), pp. 127–71.

Taylor, Rosser Howard. "Slave Conspiracies in North Carolina." *North Carolina Historical Review,* V (1928), pp. 20–34.

Wade, Richard C. "The Vesey Plot: A Reconsideration." *Journal of Southern History,* XXX, No. 2 (May 1964), pp. 143–61.

Wallace, D. D. "Social Classes and Customs in South Carolina 1830–1860." *Americana,* XXIX (1935), pp. 57–97.

Washington, Booker T. "The Free Negro in Slavery Days." *The Outlook,* XCIII (1909), pp. 107–14.

Weeks, Stephen B. "The Slave Insurrection in Virginia in

1831." *Magazine of American History*, XXV (1891), pp. 448–58.

Wesley, Charles H. "Negro Suffrage in the Period of Constitution Making, 1787–1865." *Journal of Negro History*, XXXII (1947), pp. 143–68.

Westermann, William L. "Between Slavery and Freedom." *American Historical Review*, L (January 1945), pp. 213–17.

Winston, James E. "The Free Negro in New Orleans, 1803–1860." *Louisiana Historical Quarterly*, XXI (1938), pp. 175–85.

Wish, Harvey. "American Slave Insurrections Before 1861." *Journal of Negro History*, XXII (July 1937), pp. 299–320.

INDEX

Abolitionism, 121–22, 127, 141, 144,
148–49, 162–64; agents of 127,
163–64; campaign against, 122,
149, 162–64; literature of, 162–63
Act (legislative): of 1794, 18, 160;
of 1800, 34, 45, 122, 141, 161; of
1820, 19, 28, 36, 44–45, 143, 151,
161–64; of 1822, 58, 151; of 1841,
10, 43–44, 168, 176
Adger, John, 144
African colonization. *See* American
Colonization Society; "Back to
Africa" movement; Liberia
African Meeting, 123. *See also*
A.M.E. Church
Agriculture, 56, 94–99
Allen, Richard, 123
A.M.E. (African Methodist Episco-
pal) Church, 60, 88, 123–30, 136,
140, 142–46, 153, 163. *See also*
Allen, Richard; Brown, Morris;
Church, independent black; Class
leaders; Lay preachers; Religious
community
American Colonization Society, 148,
171–78, 181. *See also* "Back to Af-
rica" movement; Liberia
American Methodist Conference,
117, 125, 128. *See also* Methodism
American Revolution, 9, 20, 52, 61,
110, 116, 150
Anglican Church. *See* Episcopal
Church. *See also* Society for the
Propagation of the Gospel
Anti-slavery sentiment, 144, 162,
173–74. *See also* Abolitionism

Artisans, free black, 38, 57, 79, 95,
98–105, 156, 174–77, 180. *See also*
Economic independence; Economic restrictions; Labor market;
Northern free blacks; Petitions,
against free blacks; Property
holders, free black; Property
rights; Rural free blacks; Taxation of free blacks

"Back to Africa" movement, 172,
174–78. *See also* American Colonization Society; Liberia
Baptist Church, 87, 110, 116, 121,
128, 144–45, 147
Benevolent Society. *See* Christian
Benevolent Society
Bennett, Gov. Thomas, 20, 135, 144,
164, 166
Blair, Francis Preston, 178
Bland, Allen, 181
Bonneau, Thomas, 73, 80, 85,
87, 94, 103, 106, 108. *See also* Education, of free blacks; Property holders; Slaveholders, free
black
Brock, Bill, 10, 42
Broughton v *Telfer*, 44
Brown Fellowship Society, 74, 81–
85, 87, 91, 107. *See also* Elite, free
black; Insurance activity
Brown, Morris, 74, 87–88, 124–31,
142–44. *See also* A.M.E. Church;
Church, independent black; Lay
preachers; Denmark Vesey, trial

213

A World in Shadow

Composed in Linotype Baskerville by Kingsport Press
with selected lines of display in Baskerville.
Printed letterpress by Kingsport Press
on Warren's University Text,
an acid-free paper noted for its longevity.
The paper was expressly watermarked
for the University of South Carolina Press
with the Press colophon.
Binding by Kingsport Press in
Elephant Hide paper
over .088 boards.